Early Praise for
100 Things I HATE/Love About Dentistry

"Dr. Samuel brilliantly reveals the realities of running a business. Her 'in your face' truths will allow you to learn from the daily tribulations, and humbly accept the triumphs that owning a business brings. Dr. Samuel's *100 Things* provides the blueprint to avoid common mistakes while maximizing your revenue. I would recommend this book to anyone who is serious about venturing out to generate income on their own terms."

-William A. Taylor, Jr., CPA, CFP®
Taylor CPA and Associates, PC
Columbus, Georgia/ Atlanta, Georgia

"*100 Things* gives an entertaining spin on real life business situations. Many of us *think* these things but don't dare say them out loud. Kudos to Dr. Samuel for capturing and exposing the experiences of most dental offices! Practicing dentistry and running a business means one must wear many different hats. Many books offer a 'how to' format for operating a business, but *100 Things* takes a hilarious look at day-to-day problems and provides viable solutions to them. Dr. Samuel's years of experience have cultivated her proven system to growing any business, making *100 Things* a MUST for the 'Business Books To Read' list!"

-Shai Hall Miles, DDS
Affordable Dentures Owner, Dothan

"This book should be ancillary reading for graduate school students. I could have used such a book five years ago. It would have been immensely helpful!"

-H. Anthony Drake, MD
Family Medicine, Board Certified

"*100 Things* is a must read for every medical professional or student who aspires to own a small business. Dr. Samuel puts a clever spin on the task of running a business, and simply put... *it WORKS!!* Dr. Samuel's simple solutions are applicable to any business!"

-Corey L. Hartman, MD, FAAD
Medical Directory, Skin Wellness Center of Alabama
Clinical Assistant Professor, Dept. of Dermatology, University of
Alabama

"All small business owners should own a copy of Dr. Samuel's *100 Things*. Implementing Dr. Samuel's straight forward systems, I saw an immediate increase in productivity!"

-Katrice L. Thomas, DMD
Private Practice Owner, Montgomery, Alabama

100 Things I HATE/Love About Dentistry

A professional's guide to efficiency, profitability, and sanity!

Dr. Evelyn Teague Samuel

Teague Principles, LLC

Teague Principles
Copyright © 2008 by Dr. Evelyn Teague Samuel All Rights Reserved
www.drevelynteaguesamuel.com

ISBN-13: 978-0-9889804-0-2
LCCN: 2013938826

Book Design by Mary Kristin Ross
Cover Image by Chuck St. John
Edited by Lisa Luckies

Printed in the United States of America

Dedication

This book is dedicated to my family: My biggest fans since birth, Mom, Bobbie Teague, and Dad, Milton Teague. To my wonderful siblings, Michael F. Teague and Telora Dean, my three astute nephews, Brandon Teague, Aaron Dean III (A.D.), and Maximus Teague (Max), along with my in-laws, James and Clara Samuel, brothers-in-law Aaron Dean II and Keith Samuel, sisters-in-law, Tinola Teague and Barbara Hall, a host of nieces and nephews through marriage, uncles, aunts, and cousins. Finally, to the love of my life, my best friend and soul mate, James Allen Samuel, Jr.

In all things that which is most important is not what we amass, not what we do, but those precious moments that are shared with the ones who know us best and love us most!

-Dr. Evelyn Teague Samuel

Contents

Acknowledgments

This book is a culmination of many years and experiences in a dental practice. Over the years, many people inspired me with stories, fuel, and content for the development of this book. My earnest appreciation and gratitude is extended to all of those who aided me in taking this from concept to fruition. Special thanks to my parents, Milton and Bobbie Teague and my siblings, Michael Teague and Telora Dean, who listened to and read countless drafts of chapters. And, much love to my husband James A. Samuel, Jr. who serves as a constant support and inspiration.

I would like to pay tribute to those who indirectly inspired me to write this book, Tom Richardson, the specialist who helped me to develop and comprise my vision for the ideal dental practice. Carlos Taylor, who told me many years ago to write a book due to my "gift of running an efficient business." My strongest dental team, Kara Phillips, Brandon Teague, Brittany Skanes, and Mia Maddox who always encouraged me to start consulting, "Because you have a gift and other doctors need your help and guidance." Finally, to the many patients who gave me the honor of being their doctor, providing the experiences and content for this book.

Lastly, I would like to express my true appreciation toward my esteemed editor, Lisa Lukies, who just seemed to "get it" in regard to my vision and manuscript, and whose attention to detail and prowess contributed to enhancing this book in a manner I only dreamt possible.

Introduction

My lifelong desire was to become a dentist... some would call it *a calling*. The first in my family to enter the field, I began predicting my future as a child. All of my quotes from elementary school through college stated that one day I would be a dentist. So, I planned my life accordingly by taking the advanced curriculum in high school and majoring in the pre-dental/pre-med curriculum in college. Fortunate to be selected to participate in a pre-dental program one summer while in college, I then went on to dental school. In fact, I was accepted into five dental schools: Marquette, Nebraska, Meharry, New Jersey, and the University of Alabama School of Dentistry (a.k.a UAB School of Dentistry). Despite vowing that I would not remain in the state of Alabama, I settled on UAB, largely due to its historically high rankings but also the strong program offered, along with the simple fact that in-state tuition could not be beaten.

Dental school was tough. People have no idea what it requires to get your D.M.D. or D.D.S. As one of our instructors used to say, "At Alabama, we don't give doctorate degrees, you earn them!" I *hated* it!!! I must have called my mom and sister every day of the four years I was in dental school, expressing my discontent. But, this was what I had wanted my entire life, and there was no Plan B. I am *not* a quitter, and failure (changing my life plan would've been just that) was not an option. I stuck it out. Surely, private practice would be different. After all, school was temporary. Life was going to be so much better once I finished school!

The day finally came when the torture was over, but what was I going to do? I had no idea where I wanted to live, how to secure a position, what kind of position to take, what pay to request, whether or not I should do a residency, and so on. I interviewed, entered the match, and undertook an Advanced Education in General Dentistry, or AEGD residency. A one-year program, I completed my residency in Washington D.C. at Howard University College of Dentistry. While I felt competent coming out of UAB's program, I thought this residency would buy some time to make life decisions while increasing my speed in treating patients. I moved to the D.C. metropolitan area (Alexandria, VA) and I must say, while I loved the metropolitan area, the cost of living was higher than what I was used to. Not to mention, residencies generally don't pay very much. I lived off credit cards—something I had never done before—amassing more debt. It is an incredible burden to be concerned about debt. I took out loans to fund my dental education, and was now taking out more loans in order to survive while in my residency! When would it ever end? But, I knew it was going to get better once I began practicing dentistry. After all, I had planned my whole life for this.

The residency came to an end. I had taken the North Eastern Regional Boards and now had a shiny, new license to practice in D.C., along with my previously-acquired Alabama license. During my residency I made a contact, an excellent clinician who I would work for along with several other offices simultaneously. Then something happened that I didn't expect... life became *tougher*. Concerned with my loan repayment kicking in along with bills and other responsibilities, I started working as an independent contractor while also working through a temp agency. I literally worked in a different office every day before eventually settling into one cosmetic dentistry office on Tuesdays and Thursdays, another HMO practice on Mondays and Wednesdays, and a third office—prosthodontist owned—on Fridays and Saturdays. I worked seven days a week, including working retail in the evenings and on weekends. It's safe to say that I am not afraid of hard work, but this was insane! Slowly, I began to resent what I was doing and question my life decisions. With all of this work, I was still barely making ends meet! So, what was it all for? After all, I had been in school for a very long time and one of the rewards should have been the ability to make a decent living. But, I reasoned, I am just starting my career, this is par for the course... one can't start off at the top. Rationalization or not, I was exhausted. There was no way I could keep up at this breakneck pace. At the time I couldn't appreciate that this experience, spending time in so many different offices, would provide my inspiration for my future practice. You learn something with each experience... what to do and what *not* to do.

Just when I felt I couldn't take any more, I received an offer to work as an associate for a group practice in Birmingham, Alabama. I struggled with the notion of moving back to a small town. Living in the most powerful city in the world, Washington D.C., had brought culture, a multitude of exposure, and countless things to do. I settled on the quality of life a smaller city offers, complete with a decreased cost of living; besides, I could always travel when and where I wanted, or so I told myself. The truth is, if it *costs* less to live in a city, you may well *make* less, and at the end of a long workweek one is not in a hurry to catch a flight to have something to do. I worked all of the time while living in D.C., but activities were at my fingertips and I had the option to partake if and when I pleased.

I moved back to Birmingham and became an associate for a group practice. There were five owners who worked short shifts (one day or evening of the week) and I was the only full time dentist. Being the only dentist was good for me, as it forced me to figure things out for myself, whether a patient or administrative issue; it also allowed me to run the clinic as if it was mine. It fell on my shoulders to come up with a recall system, collections system, and serve somewhat as a liaison between the staff and the owners. About a year into practicing with this group, I realized I wanted something greater. While I enjoyed working in an environment where I could go to another dentist for advice, the truth of the matter was that the practice was not mine. I merely worked there. When it came down to it, I had no *real* input on the direction in which the practice was going, I didn't get to make any executive decisions, and no matter what I told the staff members, they didn't have to answer to me. To top matters off, I wasn't being compensated much. So, I decided I would open my own practice.

I visualized exactly how I wanted my practice to look, run, and feel. I wrote down and researched everything I dreamed for my practice – downtown, in a high-rise professional building with panoramic views; I wanted soothing earth tone colors, light jazz, aromatherapy, a massage room, and state of the art technology. I had worked in several beautiful offices in D.C., and thought, why not bring this concept to Birmingham? So I planned... and planned... and planned.

Setting up the practice was quite a challenge. I recall going from office building to office building and being turned away. The concept of having a dental office located within a professional building is quite common in larger cities, yet it was somewhat rare in Birmingham, Alabama. I searched and searched, and, with the help of a commercial broker, was led to Park Place Towers. The space initially shown to me was on the first floor and boasted a direct view of the park. Still, I wanted to view an available space on a higher floor, and when I stepped off the elevator and glimpsed the skyline, I knew that I had found it, the home of my new practice!

Leaving no stone unturned, I consulted with the Small Business Administration where I was assigned a mentor. I won't mention his name here, but the interesting thing was that I always felt a profound sense of *"I can't"* after meeting with him. On one occasion after I had enthusiastically rattled off my ideas, he simply responded by saying, "Just because you have a new idea, doesn't mean it is a good idea." Upon returning home that day, I wrote in my journal and my entry went a little something like this: "Today I went to the small business bureau and my mentor told me that just because my idea was a new idea, it didn't mean it was a good one. Obviously, he does not know who I am, nor does he understand that everything I have chosen to do in my life, I have achieved." I never went back to the Small Business Administration, and any other person I worked with to build my practice was quickly fired, or not hired to begin with, if they could not grasp my vision.

The day finally arrived, I opened my own practice and it was everything I envisioned. Often challenging to move forward, I admit that I felt a tinge of guilt for leaving my other practice... but I knew I would never grow there and assured by the knowledge that I had done what was best for me, I allowed myself to relax. However, this beautiful, new, high-tech office came with all the responsibilities and headaches of being a small business owner. In school we were taught to be scientists, not business people. Being the consummate planner, I was prepared and hired a consulting group—the best golf player in the world has a coach, so why not employ this concept as a dentist? I have several friends who are dentists, I attend numerous continuing education courses where I mingle with colleagues from all over the country, and many dentists contact me for advice on practice procedures and office management. Throughout these processes we constantly trade battle wound stories, thus leading to this book: *The 100 Things I HATE/ Love About Dentistry*, a fun way to look at our profession. Presented as a series of occurrences or issues that crop up in the day-to-day running of a dental office, it proffers real life solutions with a positive outlook. Enjoy!

Dr. Evelyn Teague Samuel

1

Practicing Dentistry

"How can you hate practicing dentistry? This is what you do, it's your profession." I hear you ask. Let me clarify the statement, I don't hate practicing dentistry... I hate practicing dentistry in conjunction with all of the other responsibilities. I *love* practicing dentistry.

Do I sound like I am talking in riddles? Allow me to elaborate... there is a certain satisfaction that comes after completing certain procedures, especially cosmetic in nature, which may change a patient's whole demeanor, personality, and confidence level; a sense of relaxation accompanies the completion of some procedures. The issue manifests when you are focusing on so many other aspects of the dental practice that you cannot center on what is most important, dentistry.

Many dentists bemoan, "I just want to do dentistry!" And in a perfect world it would be ideal if that were all they had to concentrate on. If one has a solo practice, hiring a coach or consultant to strengthen the office systems and highly train the team will eliminate the miniscule so the doctor can then focus on the art of practicing dentistry. Problem solved.

2

Running the Business

Running the Business... Let the church say, Amen.

Dentists are skilled clinicians with great hands, artistically crafting the most beautiful anatomic design in an itty-bitty, teenie-weenie tooth. We take great joy in solving problems, alleviating our patients' pain and beautifying smiles. Many times introverts, we often go into our own worlds while working on teeth. To put it plain, we want our hands in patients' mouths.

Once, when I was filming video footage on the creation of my office, the cameraman and I were chatting about the enormity of running a business and I said, "Dentists just want their hands in patients' mouths." He could identify, stating that he "just wanted to edit film." All of the other intrinsic details take up so much time from what the profession really is.

Somewhat a freak of nature, I am a dentist who really enjoys running the business. I love figuring out the ins and outs of operations and making things run as efficiently and as smoothly as possible. I love finding a better way to do things, and I love hearing patients exclaim, "Wow this place runs so smoothly!" or "You have the best team," and "It is *so* professional here." Little do they know that things don't run smoothly on their own, many hours of training lead to the atmosphere of professionalism and the professionalism of the team.

You may not ever *love* running the business, but you can become very efficient at it. Invest in seminars, consultants, and books on business. The better you become at the business, the more time you will have to do the one thing you truly love... dentistry.

3

A Cluttered Desk

I absolutely cannot stand a cluttered desk. The truth is, a cluttered desk makes me feel extremely nervous and unsettled... I do not like disorder. Then why, you may ask, is my desk at this very moment in complete disarray? The answer to that question is simple: I have too many administrative duties. Whenever I take on too many administrative items, my desk accumulates clutter. Often times during transition, invoices, requests for narratives, and junk mail are placed on my desk. I may run to my desk in between patients to call the lab and pay a bill or shuffle papers. I have worked hard to prevent this from occurring but every now and then I slip back into old habits.

If you find that you are handling too many things that are not pertinent to your ultimate objective of providing dentistry, it is time to complete a task analysis. This is where the doctor makes a list of all of the things he/she does. The doctor then goes back and delegates tasks that can be carried out by a support team member. This facilitates doctor time being utilized for dentistry. The office administrator should be opening the mail.

Be sure to allot time for administrative duties by blocking a period on your schedule to devote to these tasks only. In my case, it is Thursday afternoon and this is the only time I work on administrative duties. My remaining office time is dedicated solely to patient care, allowing me to be focused while seeing patients.

Finally, everything on your desk should be trashed. A wise man once told me that he throws everything away, because the important things will be mailed to you again. I will be doing a desk /paper purge tomorrow! Might I suggest you do the same?

4

Disorder

Order and structure lend to professionalism. Early in my career I had the opportunity to work in many different offices, most of them were really nice and each offered me an opportunity to learn. One thing I noticed, however, was that *none* of these offices had any clear systems in place. People were hired into positions, but never trained. It was assumed that an assistant knew how to assist, a receptionist knew how to work up front, and a hygienist knew how to clean teeth. Yet, there is so much more involved with each position.

It is very important to have clear systems within the office. An office manual, complete with detailed, clear, and concise information for each position, is a must. This way, every employee knows what is expected of them, and most situations that arise can be easily handled. You will have a team that is efficient, knows their post, and doesn't come to the doctor for every little thing. Instead of disorder, you will have an environment of order.

5

The Art of Delegation

Ever had a day where everybody came to you for every little thing? One of those days where each team member had to ask you how to do something, or how to tell a patient something about their account, or how to handle something, or how to fix something, etc.? A day where you gave specific instructions on a project, only to have a team member come back to you twenty times asking what to do next; making you want to scream, "If I am doing every step through you, it would be much easier to do it myself!" And you can't help but wonder, "If I have to do everything, what the Sam Hill am I paying my team for?"

Having to think for everybody in the office is most exhausting. With all that you already have on your mind, you are now literally thinking through each team member's processes. Think about it, if you have to do everything, why do you pay others a salary? Train the team, and if they cannot handle tasks without having you do the assignment, hire more proficient team members. If you have a solid team, you should be able to delegate, which brings me to a delicate issue for most dentists... the fine art of delegation.

Dentists, or any business owner, should master the craft of delegation. Truth be told, we dentists are such extreme perfectionists that we often do not. No one can do the task at hand with the level of skill and precision that we have, and chances are you are correct in assuming this. However, we cannot and should not do it all... unless you want a one-way ticket to the funny farm. I know in your mind's eye right now you are flicking through all of the past assignments you granted where each step was brought back to you for your opinion. All of those moments where you realized it would be easier and quicker to just do it yourself. Despite this, we must relinquish the need to control all. Delegate. Delegate. Delegate.

6

Running Behind

I hate to keep people waiting; however, when I frequent other businesses this does not appear to be the norm. Constantly paying attention to customer service everywhere I go is the result—or curse! —of owning a service-oriented business. Paying close attention to how employees greet customers, their interest in the customer and their job, how they move (fast or lethargically), their attitude in general, and most importantly, how far behind they are running occurs very naturally each time I enter a business. Sadly, I don't think I have ever received the level of care our office gives at other establishments (possibly due to my own OCD). Each place I visit and observe bad business habits, I want to stop everything and coach them… or shake them... or shake them first and then coach them. You get the picture.

Running behind makes me nervous. I do not like to wait, and I do not like for others to wait on me. This is why I always run on time. It is with utter dismay that I witness many of my colleagues running habitually late, either by loading schedules way too tight or merely arriving to work late, resulting in patients waiting.

The best advice I can offer? STOP! Stop scheduling the book too tight, stop coming to work late, and *STOP* running behind. Use the golden rule, *"Do unto others as you would have them do unto you."* Beyond common courtesy, you will feel less frazzled when your office runs on schedule, instantly transforming its energy from chaos to harmony.

7

Running on Roller Skates

Or running around like a chicken with its head cut off! …
However you want to state it. The office can seem frenetic at times, especially if the appointment book is chock-full. Have you ever had days where you must've seen at least one thousand mouths only to review your reports at the end of the day and realize that you were not productive at all? Too many patients, due to poor scheduling, can be extremely stressful. It will lead the clinical team to being dog tired by the end of the day, add to mistakes being made, and cause the office to run behind.

One of my biggest pet peeves is to run behind. Block scheduling will resolve the zoo house, allowing patients to be treated efficiently and the doctor to complete more procedures on fewer patients. Better scheduling tactics allow for emergency patients without disruption to the day. Each day goes by smoother, the office is more productive and you will be able to focus on quality instead of quantity in regards to treating your patients. No roller skates required.

8

Scrubs

Many dental and medical offices wear scrubs for office attire. This is a way to make sure that everyone in the office is identifiable. It makes things easy for the team in regards to figuring what to wear every day, provides uniformity and is, let's face it, just what health care facilities wear. It looks medical and official... or does it?

Throughout the years I have found, quite frankly, that scrubs just don't look neat. Sure, everyone has on the same color—and some are cute—but often times they are wrinkled, faded, and not presentable. In the past, when I was required to wear scrubs, I found that I too was guilty of being so comfortable that I would throw my hair in a knot in the morning, not put on any make up and head out the door. Now, there is nothing wrong with wearing your hair up if you are a female and not wearing makeup if you like being natural. But for me, it was just a bit too comfortable. Kind of like those people who fly commercial airlines in pajamas – in the middle of the day!

Dressing nice commands attention. For example, there are times when we run out to the grocery store or a nice clothing store in a rush and just throw on the first thing we can grab, let's say jeans and a tee. Then there are times when we may visit that same grocery store or nice clothing store very well dressed. If you have never done this try an experiment and dress oppositely and see the response. It is inevitable that the sales representatives will be more attentive when you are in nice attire. One of the first things I teach my team upon initial employment is never judge a book by its cover, and while we try not to do this in our office, many people in this world do. Nice attire conveys that you are sharp, serious, successful, and that you will buy. Hence the age old quote, "Dress for success" or "Dress for the career you want to have"... and so on.

Apply *dressing for success* to the dental office. Picture a dentist entering the room and discussing a large and involved case with you. Would you pay more attention to the dentist wearing scrubs? Or would the dentist wearing a shirt, tie and white coat convey more professionalism? A majority of patients will recognize the person in the more professional attire as authoritative, sharp, intelligent, on top of their game, successful... well, you get my drift. It looks good and it sets you apart from the norm. In our office we wore designer lab jackets in all black, they looked chic and we didn't look like your typical dental office. Dress for the practice you want to have!

9

Checking Hygiene

It is often little things that add stress to your life. Who knew, way back in dental school while mastering the basics during sophomore year when we actually got to go inside the dental clinics and physically work our first procedures on each other—cleaning teeth—that such a simple procedure would create stress later in life. Allow me to elaborate: no dentist likes to clean teeth! In fact, I am going to go out on a limb and say that we all *hate* cleaning teeth! Hate is a rather strong word, but most dentists *would* prefer to be doing other dental procedures, which is why we have hygienists. I employed a wonderful hygienist, but even with a great—and wonderful—hygienist, the hygiene check requires the doctor to stop whatever procedure he or she is working on to go and check another patient. When working on a patient, your mind is on the subject at hand. To stop mid procedure requires a refocus of your energy to give attention to another patient, different teeth, different dental conditions, and a different personality.

Hygiene checks usually don't take very long, yet they prove to be quite disruptive. And, sometimes when you do the check, you get a "talker" and it can be difficult to get out of the room and back to the patient you were treating in your main operatory. Remedy this by templating your schedule—I mention the imperative use of block scheduling in several chapters, and in conjunction, the same method should be applied to the hygiene book: schedule long hygiene procedures such as periodontal therapy simultaneously with long doctor procedures. This will prevent you from stopping your treatment numerous times. Scheduling longer routine hygiene appointments (e.g. one hour, even though most hygiene appointments do not necessarily take that long) allows the hygienist to spend ample time with each patient without being rushed. This also allows the doctor to come in and complete a timely examination of the patient, and the patient to finish their appointment well before the estimated hour. It is a win-win for all parties involved and evokes a sense of professionalism for the office.

10

Adjusting Occlusion

Tap, tap, tap... grind... adjust. Tap, tap, tap... grind... adjust. Tap, tap, tap... grind... adjust. Sound monotonous? Adjusting occlusion or, in laymen terms, adjusting the bite—tap, tap, tap and slide side to side—is a part of dentistry. Any time a restoration (filling, crown, or appliance) is done, the bite must be checked to make sure the patient feels as normal as possible. Due to the periodontal ligament, or PDL, the patient will feel the slightest variation. As precise as we are as dentists and as close as we may get, nothing is better than what the patient had prior to needing dental work... or better stated, than what the Good Lord gave them.

The issue is when we must take large amounts of time to make sure the bite is right; for example, porcelain restorations (crowns, inlays, bridges, etc.) that require excessive adjusting. This is a rarity in my practice, as early on I learned the importance of using quality dental laboratories. You get what you pay for (in all aspects of life), and while you may think you are saving money by using a less expensive lab, if that lab is sending cases that require an enormous amount of time to place and adjust, you are losing revenue. You are adjusting away all that expensive porcelain and using up more chair time. Remedy this by sourcing a high quality lab and brushing up on your impression and bite index skills. And you'll be saying "tap, tap, tap.... grind... slide from slide to slide" a lot less often.

11

Writing Up Charts

Writing charts is very necessary for standard patient care; it can also protect both you and the patient legally. The downside to maintaining detailed patient charts is that it can become time consuming, making it easy to fall behind on them. This is especially true if you go straight from one patient to the next running to stay on schedule.

The easy solution is going paperless. Investing in good office computer software such as Dentrix or Eaglesoft is imperative, allowing you to automatically write up charts upon checking patients out. Have your assistant check patients out in the treatment room and program the computer to automatically write the chart. Your assistant can add anything you did differently (i.e. one more carpule of anesthesia, etc.), and you would approve and sign off on the entry. Any additional treatment involved would still need to be written by the doctor, but compared with writing the entire chart manually, dental office software programs are a gift from the technology gods!

Time saving aside, I cannot stress how important it is to document in great detail. Document like you are defending yourself in court. Maintaining detailed charts will protect both you and your patient.

12

Accounts Receivable

Accounts Receivable is outstanding monies for procedures
that you have provided but have not yet received payment for. There are a couple
of main reasons your practice may have funds that you have not received, one
being that you are a preferred provider for insurance carriers. When dealing
with insurance companies, it is not uncommon for offices to amass large
accounts receivable. You do the work and the patient pays some arbitrary
co-pay, based on an estimate you receive from the insurance company. You
send the claim to the insurance company and they mull over whether or not
they will pay you. In some cases, they make you write numerous narratives
begging them to pay you and request you submit countless x-rays to justify
that the prescribed treatment was necessary for your patient. And, if you are
lucky, you will receive a payment some thirty days after you have done the
work. Sometimes several months will pass, and in other situations you are
calling and calling about payment for work you've already done, only to give
up! I think most insurance companies are banking on this, hence the calcu-
lated delays. After all this work you end up writing off a huge chunk of your
fees—a loss that you agree to accept when you sign your name—*in blood*—
on a contract with the insurance company, in exchange for them promoting
your name and sending you insurance-driven patients.

Another cause for large accounts receivable is allowing patients to have
work done and then "billing" them… *Good luck!* You will see the rest of that
payment when hell freezes over! I've witnessed dentists complete extensive
work for a patient to pay only $50 a month (for a lifetime) because the patient

was having a hard time, etc. Well, guess what? *You* will be having a hard time when your practice loan is due, your team needs to be paid, and a multitude of other financial responsibilities need to be taken care of. Vendors are not going to let you pay when you "get the money." You must set the tone. If you are constantly billing the patient or letting the patient pay what they can afford, after providing and covering lab costs on your all-so-expensive dentistry, then you are enabling people to treat you just as they do! Without clear guidelines in place, expecting patients to act any other way would be insanity on your part.

Some dentists see large accounts receivable as a good thing. I recall a conversation with a colleague at the close of one year in which I told her, "This year my accounts receivable is much lower." I went on to explain that my numbers (collections) were better that year, meaning I did not have large receivables going into the following year. Her response? "Evelyn that's not good! If I don't have accounts receivable, to me that means there is no growth!" Aye-ya-ya! *What?!* I didn't quite understand this. Had I not just told her that my collections had shot up from the year prior and I didn't have large accounts receivable? HELLO!!! This means I got paid for the work I did. No accounts receivable means that patients and insurance companies don't owe outstanding payments that are often impossible to collect. No accounts receivable means we didn't work for free this year people! Comprende?

It is *very* important to get payment at the time dental services are provided. In cases that require large blocks of scheduling, our office collects at the time the appointment is made. This decreases the instances of no shows or broken appointments. If a patient cannot pay when scheduling an appointment, chances are they will not be able to pay you for the same procedure in a couple of days. The difference is literally a day or two. When done correctly, block scheduling usually allows patients requiring large procedures to be booked right away. Given this convenience and the fact that patients are seen on time and have more one-on-one time with the doctor, most willingly comply with this payment requirement. Accounts receivable decreases, everyone is happy, and all is good with the world! After all, isn't payment in your account today much better than a payment you may or may not receive tomorrow?

13

Numbers

Or should I say *evaluating* numbers? In every business numbers and the evaluation of them are essential. The numbers consist of services that generate cash flow (collections or actual currency that has been collected for services provided) and accounts receivable (monies outstanding, which have not been collected for services provided). Obviously, accounts receivable are undesirable. Offices can get bogged down producing, but production means nothing but free dental work if collections are not secured. There *are* ways to collect for your services. How do you do *that?* Very simple... you ask for payment!

Sounds oversimplified, I know, but it truly is key. The majority of customers do not pay because they were never presented firm financial arrangements from the get go. Without a clear understanding of their insurance, they may not realize that no insurance company truly pays 100%. And quite frankly, Dr. Work-For-Free, no one informed them or asked them for payment. Why is it okay not to pay the dentist? *It is NOT okay!*

Establish firm financial arrangements for the office. Remember, you went to school to be a dentist and help patients, you ARE NOT a banker. Third party financing should therefore be available, and in the event that a bank/lender will not extend credit to the patient, you shouldn't either. If the banks can't collect, what makes you think you can?

Always secure payment up front for large blocks reserved on the doctor's book. Airlines, spas, hotels, and even some restaurants require a credit card reservation prior to arrival, why not the dentist? Never, *EVER*, allow team members to schedule large procedures or blocks of the doctor's time without collecting the fee at time of scheduling. In my experience, patients who prepay for large services show up for their appointments, and in instances where prepayment was not collected, broken appointments increased. Nothing good comes out of the doctor losing this kind of production time.

Educate your team on the concept of exchange and be sure they understand that you deserve to be paid for your services. How many places, besides healthcare facilities such as dental offices, can you buy something and not have to pay for it at time of purchase? In the event that you have a team member who continuously chooses not to collect payment, you will need to evaluate whether that person is an asset or liability to your practice.

Patients generally don't have a problem with this policy and people feel good about honoring their financial obligations. This collection process benefits all involved, resulting in improved customer relations, fewer complaints, and most importantly, increased profitability.

14

Bills, Bills, Bills... and More Bills!

Having a dental practice undoubtedly brings about bills, from practice rent or mortgage to supplies. Bills at the beginning of the month, bills in the middle of the month, and, yep, you guessed it, bills at the end of the month! It is not uncommon for a dentist to numb a patient and then run to their office to pay bills during the short time the anesthesia takes effect. There are *so* many bills that one may think, "Are you serious, another one?" as they continuously roll in month after month after month. The minutia in itself is a headache, and the volume at which they arrive, a migraine!

You are probably thinking, "Well, Dr. Teague, I can identify with what you are saying, but what do you suppose we do? This is not something that can be changed?" And yes, you are right to an extent. We cannot change the fact that we have a huge financial obligation, but we can adjust the way we approach this responsibility. Instead of focusing on how much debt we have, we can focus on how our investment in ourselves, and our practice, will bring financial freedom. Instead of focusing on another bill, think "another payment" as they come in. Instead of running to pay bills in between patients or while patients are numbing, set aside time to handle invoices. This will allow you to focus entirely on patients as you are working. Better still, have your bookkeeper or accountant pay your invoices. A note to the wise, in the event that you do hire someone to pay your invoices, may I suggest—despite adding a task to your long list of tasks—that you always sign your own checks... I'll elaborate why in another chapter.

15

Overhead

Overhead, or the cost of running your business, is one, if not the single most stressful aspect of dentistry. Dental practices surpass many other medical professions in terms of overhead. The equipment required, along with the supplies and materials necessary to perform, is often exorbitant. This is in conjunction with lab fees for patient restorations (crowns, etc.). Given this very expensive office needs to provide nurturing people to care for its patients—and in most cases, these people do like to be paid—one must also factor the cost of the team into the equation.

It is estimated that most practices in the U.S operate, on average, with about 75% overhead. In case you have trouble with math, let me break that down for you: for every dollar you produce, you get twenty-five cents. Whoop! I don't know one person who would work at a laborious job all week long for just twenty-five cents on a dollar. When you are looking at costs of $40k a month (on a conservative estimate) or much higher just to keep your doors open, prior to the doctor getting paid a dime, the question may enter your mind, "Why didn't I pick another area of medicine?" No matter how much you love creating healthy smiles or performing artwork (because it truly is art!), it is not enough if you are not reaping the financial rewards. Or simply put, getting *paid*.

Be vigilant with overhead and find out the breakdown of your percentages. Check with your supply companies and other reputable sources about the breakdown of your overhead. A good accountant will also be able to tell you if your averages are out of sync. Cutting back on overhead may include downsizing your team. Offices are often over-staffed with positions that could easily be handled by fewer and more efficient individuals. Decreasing your overhead will alleviate a portion of stress and allow you, the doctor, to GET PAID!!! After all, nothing in life is free and *you* should not work for free!

16

Insurance

Insurance. What is insurance? According to *Wikipedia*, the free online encyclopedia, insurance is:

"In law and economics, insurance is a form of risk management primarily used to hedge against the risk of a contingent, uncertain loss. Insurance is defined as the equitable transfer of the risk of a loss, from one entity to another, in exchange for payment. An insurer is a company selling the insurance; an insured, or policyholder, is the person or entity buying the insurance policy. The insurance rate is a factor used to determine the amount to be charged for a certain amount of insurance coverage, called the premium. Risk management, the practice of appraising and controlling risk, has evolved as a discrete field of study and practice."

The one thing I hate most about dentistry is insurance. Now don't get me wrong, it has its place and people do need health care, but the fact that these companies have CEO's who get paid millions of dollars a year with perks and stocks for even more millions and millions is beyond me. The average maximum rate of dental benefits granted to patients in 1960 was $1000 per year. Now, some fifty years later, patients still average—drum roll, please—$1000 per year maximum dental benefits! You don't have to be a genius to figure that costs have exponentially inflated over the last fifty years. Why then would a patient still receive this nominal amount toward their dental care?

Adding insult to injury, insurance companies can tell a network provider that he must discount his fees up to 50% or more.... it is ludicrous. Does this same dentist, or network provider, receive a discount on supplies, rent or utilities? Can he or she pay the dental team half of their wages? Can he or she provide the quality—and I emphasize, *QUALITY*—care at half the cost? Heck, let me go one step further, can the dentist make a decent living? It costs hundreds of thousands of dollars to become a dentist and if one owns a practice, hundreds of thousands more. Why then, should an insurance company with CEO's raking in multi-millions and coders with no medical training dictate what your treatment is worth? The simple answer... *THEY SHOULD NOT!*

I am not suggesting that you don't accept insurance. I am demonstrating that we, the dentists are not the beneficiaries of the contract with the insurance companies. An in-network contract demands that you reduce your fees, and there would not be plans like this if dentists did not sign up for them. A better option is to have patients pay for treatments at the time of service and (as a courtesy) file the insurance claims on their behalf. The insurance company then pays the patient directly, taking your office out as the middleman. After all, the patient is paying this insurance company for a policy. Using this approach, you are no longer required to work for half of your fees. How many people do you know would go to work all day and accept being paid half of their salary or wages? I know... not one! So why should dentists?

17

David and Goliath

I was surfing the net to get an idea of what dental insurance companies pay their CEOs; my curiosity piqued by the fact that insurance companies dictate how much dentists should charge for their services. To my surprise, much of the compensation is public knowledge and readily available. During my search, I came across an in-depth article and video footage from a news station revealing tax information for the nation's largest provider of dental insurance. According to this source, this particular insurance company has 56 million patients in its network—about one-third of all dental patients in the country. During the year of 2009, numerous executives at this company made in excess of three million dollars. The company also offered a host of benefits such as exclusive memberships in addition to covering travel expenses for the executives' spouses. Astounding but true, one can pull up the tax information online to verify these numbers. The year 2010 was much the same and the executives' salaries and bonuses (some of which quadrupled their base salaries) were verifiable on their tax information. For example: One executive listed showed a salary of $659,608 in addition to a bonus of $789,500! Now, I don't know about you, but I don't know any dentists raking in that kind of dough treating patients. Who is the giant here?

So how can this *Goliath* state that the dentist is charging too much for a crown? In the insurance world, this would be worded as "providers fees are above UCR" (usual, customary, and reasonable or covered charges). Let us say the fee for the crown is $950. If you are a network provider "in network," the insurance company may dictate you charge $569. I have clearly conveyed how much overhead occurs within a dental practice. Now, factor in up to two appointments (chair time) for crown preparation and crown delivery, lab expenses, supplies required, materials used, and team members to pay. Does not leave much room for profit, does it? While we are here to serve and help patients, to remain in business we must make a profit. There is no way to recoup the loss for the difference between your costs and the fee the insurance company contracted you to charge.

We all know the biblical story of David and the giant Goliath. Without being clad in armor, David defeated Goliath with a single, slingshot-propelled stone to the forehead. Goliath fell to the ground and David finished him off. Far be it for me to say that we dentists could use a slingshot, but, united we stand and divided we fall. As stated before, the insurance restrictive plans and fee schedules would not exist if dentists refused to sign up for them.

18

Broken Appointments

It never ceases to amaze me that patients come into the office for the first visit, fill out and sign paperwork clearly citing office policies, namely the highlighted section that reads *THERE WILL BE A $50 FEE ASSESSED FOR APPOINTMENTS CANCELLED WITHOUT 48 HOURS NOTICE,* not to mention, upon leaving the office viewing a beautiful and modern wood-framed sign that reads the same... and still break numerous appointments.

There are different schools of thought on the broken appointment fee. Many dentists fear that assessing a penalty for what is clearly a bold assassination of their schedule, will invoke anger in the offender, thus resulting in him (the offender) never returning to the office. Others fear assessing fees leads to the offender getting upset and filing a lawsuit.

Another school of thought is that this act should not go unpunished. Such belief stems from a scenario that goes a little something like this: Patient presents to clinic for initial appointment. Patient signs agreement that fees will be assessed if future appointments are broken without giving proper notice (usually 24 or 48 hours). Patient schedules next appointment. Patient is a no show and a no call for appointment. Patient calls back the next day, "Hello, this is Ms. I-Forgot and I had an appointment yesterday. I am *so* sorry, but I forgot. Can you please reschedule me? I really need to have my teeth fixed." Receptionist is forgiving and puts Ms. I-Forgot back on the schedule. Next appointment rolls around. Ms. I-Forgot calls one hour before and says, "I am *so* sorry I had an office meeting I couldn't miss", or, "I forgot... again", or, "my dog ate my appointment card"... REALLY!!!

After tolerating countless Ms. I-Forgots, demonstrating an absolute disrespect to office policy, many dentists, and other health professionals, began to assess fees. Of course there will be emergencies, and most offices will take those into consideration, but the amount of revenue lost when a patient consistently refuses to take responsibility for their actions is nauseating. Many patients adopt the attitude, "Oh they can just see someone else." Well, we can't just see someone else at the last minute when that time slot was reserved for you, Ms. I-Forgot! We don't have a waiting room full of stand-bys!

Numerous no shows, over the course of time, result in an enormous loss of revenue. I know, I know, all doctors are RICH and can absorb those costs. Based on their HIGH prices they can clearly afford it! ... If only that was the truth. No-shows result in that time slot being lost forever. It can never be made up. Without notice, no other person can take that slot and the overhead still has to be met (team, utilities, rent/mortgage, etc.). This is detrimental for any small business.

My office block schedules, meaning we spend one-on-one time with each patient. This also means when a patient walks in the door, he or she barely gets the chance to sit in the reception area before being called for their appointment. Yes, that's right... patients *do not* wait. When scheduling this way, there is low traffic flow and the office remains quiet and serene, but for it to work effectively, it is important that patients show up for appointments. The alternative is scheduling so tight that patients have to wait extended periods of time for appointments, usually resulting in the office team becoming frazzled because the place is a madhouse - all in an attempt to account for patients that may not show. For me, over scheduling is not worth it. I value the time I spend with my patients and I value our (the team's) sanity.

Options to counter the broken appointment are: Assessing a fee (mind you, $50 will not cover the overhead for the time lost), requesting a credit card to hold the reservation at time of scheduling (hotels do it!), or scheduling too tight (chasing your tail). My office combines options. We require full payment at time of scheduling for large block appointments or major procedures. This definitely decreases the amount of no-shows, and with this option, patients are usually seen within a couple of days. We *do* assess the broken appointment fee, and we do not reschedule habitual offenders. We send email and text message reminders two days prior (48-hr window, thus providing an out) and another reminder one hour before the appointment. We send post card reminders, and we provide courtesy calls. There is no excuse—*I forgot*—to forget!

19

Cold Hard Sales

Salespeople abound, and not only in dentistry, who will sell you products they don't even believe in just to clinch a sale. They will visit your office and read a study—conducted by their own company—depicting their product as the best thing since sliced bread. Usually my eyes glaze over as they paint a picture of green pastures and blue skies, cherry blossoms in full bloom, with the wind gently blowing in my hair as I take in a serene lake with a perfect rainbow arching across it. No, wait! ... Make that *two* rainbows stretching across the azure sky with a pot of gold at the end of each that's mine for the taking! I hate to be sold.

The cold sell, whereby salespeople pick up the phone, call the office and try to make a sale with no establishment of rapport is probably the least effective and most annoying tactic. My next least favorite is the hard sell, where the salesperson comes in and attempts to intimidate you into buying. For example: A saleswoman numerous years ago was scheduled to come and sell me an oral cancer screening system. She spoke very loud and was uncontrollably animated. Her boss had come on this appointment in tandem, unannounced, which bothered me even further. Ms. Hard Sell kept repeating, "Your office is so nice I can't believe you don't have this system" etc. I found her highly inappropriate, I mean, wasn't that the purpose of her being there? So the office *would* have it. Like myself, my team was fairly laid back and calm, which only illuminated how obnoxiously loud and out of control Ms. Hard Sell was. Her inability to know her audience and in essence mirror them was painfully obvious; if she had paid the least bit attention to me, the buyer, she would've known to stop the sales jargon and simply provide the facts and literature as I had already researched the product prior to the appointment. This particular salesperson was more concerned with showing her boss that she could deliver a hard sales pitch, and her pushy, boisterous behavior almost cost her the sale.

What makes me an expert on sales you might ask? Good question. What makes me an expert is that I sell daily. I have also read numerous books and attended countless seminars on the topic. We are all in sales, especially in dentistry. Many doctors will have their hair stand on end to hear "sales" referred to in conjunction with health care, but it is what it is. EVERY THING YOU DO IS SALES. When you present yourself in a positive professional way, you are selling, and when you efficiently run your practice, you are selling. That also applies in reverse, negative presentation and inefficient running of the practice, albeit poor, you are selling. Even the way you speak—*Yep! You betcha!*—you're still selling.

Read as many books as you can on selling and remember most people buy or work with people because they like them and have a sense of trust for them. Any form of pressure is a sure fire way to lose business.

20

Being Tech Support

Isn't it utterly annoying when everyone comes to you for *everything*? Don't you have enough responsibilities? Well, in addition to all of those responsibilities and tasks you are also tech support, congratulations. Being tech support means when anything breaks, malfunctions, or just plain doesn't work, you will hear the words, "Doctor? This doesn't work," or, "Doctor? This is leaking," or, "Doctor? The hand piece is out again," or, "Doctor? The x-ray arm is drifting," or, "Doctor? The patient light is drifting," or, "Doctor? The patients say they can't feel the nitrous," or, "Doctor? The copy machine is printing funny," or, "Doctor? The paper won't stop coming out on the check machine," or, "Doctor? Doctor? Doctor? Doctor?"... Get the point?

I bet you didn't know you would be responsible for fixing everything from the x-ray head to the DSL? I wish I could offer a solution to this but the reality is, as the Chief Executive Officer, it is ultimately your responsibility. Of course, systems need to be put in place to minimize the number of times people come to you with these issues: utilize a great IT company, a good supply company with equipment technicians, a maintenance man, and team members with the common sense to make decisions without coming to you. For example, if you have special overhead lights and one is blown, a team member should figure out that maintenance needs to replace the light bulb without you having to instruct them to have it replaced.

21

I'm Sorry We Can't Fix That

With the massive amount of equipment required in dentistry, things will inevitably go wrong. Better stated, machinery breaks down. The part that I take issue with is when the equipment is relatively new, goes on the blink, and the first solution from tech support is "You need to replace it", or "I'm sorry we can't fix that." Nonsense! I cannot count the times that I have been instructed to replace a piece of equipment as a first line of defense, and just about each time—with a little persistence—the problem has been resolved … without having to replace it!

For example, about three years after I opened my practice, we began experiencing problems with the x-ray machine in operatory room one: the arm was drifting like crazy, preventing us from making timely radiographs. My office personnel contacted the equipment maintenance person from the company who sold me all of my large equipment and instruments. Sounds simple enough, right? Fixing the arm of a three-year old machine to prevent movement in the short 2 seconds it takes to step out of the room and shoot an x-ray. After all, most x-ray units last for a number of years – I've seen some as old as twenty years, albeit outdated but functioning. I will make a long story short, equipment maintenance personnel called the manufacturer's support who could not locate the part needed and the only way to remedy the problem would be to purchase a new machine. Ahem. Let's see, it would cost me $5000 to purchase a new machine to replace the three-year old one I had only just bought... "I don't think so, Homie don't play that"! Bypassing all of the middlemen who had only served to prevent progress, I spoke with the equipment specialist who aided the setup of my office, and like magic, the correct part for my x-ray arm arrived, the repair carried out and the arm worked like new within a couple of short weeks. And, there was no additional charge to me as the machine was still considered new!

My number one suggestion is to remain persistent. If the person you are dealing with cannot solve your problem, find someone who can. I am not saying that things will not need to be replaced from time to time. I am saying however, that others do stand to make a profit at the expense of your "lack of knowledge" or more bluntly, "ignorance"! Do your research and make sure that all efforts are being made to repair something before it is trashed and replaced.

22

Everything is an Emergency

From the patient who has a toothache and wakes up like a sleeping bear, starts to hurt and must be addressed immediately–the same patient you diagnosed six months ago but who neglected to follow through with treatment; to the sales people calling and calling to get on your book; to the patient needing to be numbed in hygiene; to the person on the phone who wants to ask the doctor a question ... *EVERYTHING* is an "emergency."

BUT, IT IS NOT!

Each person we encounter feels his issue is an emergency. The doctor is but one person, and some things can—*and have to*—wait. There are *urgencies* and then there are *emergencies*. Urgencies require attention, but emergencies require immediate attention. Educate your team on the differences so they are able to filter correctly.

23

Emergency Patients

Emergency patients can wreck the flow of the schedule, resulting in patients with appointments having to wait. Never let an emergency cause a scheduled patient to wait. It was paramount for my office to run on time and one of the features my patients valued the most. For this reason I strongly emphasize having a contingency plan in place for emergency patients. Emergencies will occur and we want to be available for those who require these services, but we must handle them proficiently. Have you ever been to an emergency room and waited for hours on top of hours? Not fun. This is not something that any party enjoys, not the emergency patient, not the patient with the appointment made months ago, or the team.

To facilitate the patient with a true emergency, clear blocks on the schedule and set those aside for such occurrences. This will allow the office to quickly schedule in the emergency patient and prevent others from waiting. In the event that you do not have room for an emergency patient on your schedule—which should rarely happen if you have blocks set aside— refer to a local emergency dental clinic.

That being said, I must add that there are not very many true dental emergencies, there are however numerous urgencies. An emergency is extreme discomfort, an avulsed tooth, etc. Urgencies are something that may hurt but are not bad – such as, "my temporary came off" or "I broke a filling but have no associated pain," "I cracked something" or "I chipped something". To the patient everything seems like an emergency. Train your staff to differentiate between a true emergency and urgencies.

24

Emergency Mode

What is "Emergency Mode" and what circumstances
warrant the switch to Emergency Mode?

Emergency Mode is a mode one goes into when the bottom line or practice numbers become dangerously and uncomfortably low. Circumstances will arise in any business causing the need to kick into emergency mode. When I first launched my practice I went over budget on my build-out and had virtually no working capital remaining, cue, Emergency Mode. Other examples would be if you left for extended periods of time to partake in continuing education courses, or an empty schedule due to vacation periods or inclement weather, etc. Whatever the reason, Emergency Mode will need to be implemented.

Entering Emergency Mode, I become extremely focused on turning things around. Coming up with creative ideas, working longer hours and brushing up on the efficiency of the practice, and one of my main contingency plans is heavy marketing. Most old school dentists believe marketing is taboo; back in the day, a dentist would hang his shingle on the door and—*abracadabra*—patients appeared. We now live in an age where marketing is absolutely necessary. Dentists are not a commodity; a dentist is not a dentist is not a dentist and there must be an avenue for patients to know you are in practice! Potential patients need to know that you have completed extensive courses and training and offer services that set you apart from other practices. Shout it from the rooftops! How else will they ever find you?

A wise saying I once heard, "When things are good you should market, and when things are bad you *must* market." I couldn't agree more, if you pull back when things are slow no one will know you're there. In a time of decrease it is really important for patients to know who you are, where you are, and what services you provide. Off you go to the rooftop now with a megaphone in hand!

25

Gloom and Doom

Since I began working on this book four years ago, our economy lurched into a downward spiral. Right at the start of this economic madness, I employed consultants whom I had chosen based on their life philosophy – with an emphasis on living life and allowing work to follow. While some ideas they preached may seem hokey or simplistic to most— and I refer to some of these tactics throughout this book—I discovered that they really work. People like to feel good! You could sell pie in the sky and, if it sounds good and gives hope, people will buy it… I did!

Our entire office team returned from seminars empowered and inspired, feeling like we could do anything. Striving hard to maintain our sense of positivism, we protected ourselves from negativity by entering what I like to call the bubble. Patients would come in talking about the economy, which we would counter with something positive; we stopped watching the news (not so great for keeping up-to-date with current affairs, but definitely good for remaining in the bubble). The media brings much sensationalism and negativity, so we avoided it like the plague and it worked! Many businesses began declining as my business began flourishing. Astounding!

Fast forward to today, where I find myself on the coattails of a week that has been tediously slow to say the least, throwing my team into somewhat of a frenzy. More patients than usual complained about costs and even I went into a slight state of delirium because the overhead doesn't stop just because the book slows. Like a dark, ominous cloud, a heavy sense of loss of control hung over my entire team. Tales of previous employers filing bankruptcy or closing their practices spread rapidly through the office, and everybody was saying, "It is so bad, I'm scared." Usually level headed, I found myself internalizing many of the fearful comments and began to FREAK OUT... not my standard method for handling situations.

As a leader it is important to stay focused and remain the voice of reason so, checking myself, I took a deep breath and handled our office meltdown in true Dr. Teague style. Meeting each team member one-on-one in my office I asked, "Are you okay?" giving them the opportunity in private to express any fears, I then went on to assure each one of them that our office would be fine and encouraged them not to get caught up in the "fear factor." Most dialogue with my team members revealed a united fear of turning away price shoppers and insurance-driven patients given the schedule was slow. Immediately referring to our office purpose which states, "We only see people who value our services," I pointed out something that my staff already knew, many of those price shoppers, or "D" patients, would not be returning for services anyway. Our office mission and purpose did not allow for those who do not value our services. In order to survive as a business, we needed to remain true to our mission, regardless of what the books were showing.

So when times get tough, and inevitably periods of difficulty arise in any business, I invite you to allow me to talk you off the cliff. Imagine you can hear my voice, soft, encouraging and soothing... "I invite you into the bubble. Stay in the bubble. Know that everything will work out and you will be fine. The downfall of others is not an indicator of what can happen to you, you are great! Capable of unimaginable, magnificent things, you are anything you wish to be! You are a living legend in the making." Believe me... it works!

26

Negativity

Negativity spreads like an infectious disease whether it initiates from the patient, the team, or the doctor. Metaphysical beliefs such as the "law of attraction" or "like attracts like" do exist and factual or not, it simply *feels* better when one elects to be positive. My team focuses on the positives. When I began writing this book, the state of the economy had only just begun its historic decline. During tough periods, especially the economic downturn in 2008, I intentionally focused our office meetings on positivism; completing our role-playing exercises on treatment, treatment plan, and financial option presentations as if patients would accept each case. And an interesting thing happened; our office began to do better than the year prior despite the declining economic state. I introduced reading material in the form of positive books and posted positive quotes on the board in our break room. Whenever a patient recited tales of doom and gloom during appointments, we directed the conversation to a more positive topic, often changing the tone of the patient and allowing them to adopt a better outlook!

And in true law-of-attraction style, whenever we relaxed our training in this category and allowed negativity to rear its ugly head, we noticed the direct impact and difference it made to our circumstances. Therefore, it is important to promote and maintain the concept of positivism as an imperative aspect in your office training.

27

Murphy's Law

Ever awakened on the wrong side of the bed? What the heck is the wrong side of the bed anyway? My sentiment is that if you didn't wake up on the floor after rolling off, either side is the right side. But we all know the type of day that inspired this expression...

It is the day you slept late due to the power going off in the middle of the night, the alarm clock not chiming (all before cell phones) and realized you were going to be LATE. Typically this would also be the day that you had a big case scheduled. And we all know, if you start off behind it sets the stage for the entire day. You get up, shower and throw on the first items of clothing you can find before realizing that you cannot find your keys (adding another 15 minutes to your commute). Finally arriving at the office, you discover the big case is not in from the lab, but your patient has shown up for his appointment.

Now in all the years I have been practicing, I rarely ever raised my voice or lost my temper. All of my employees knew the one thing that would make me an unhappy camper, and that would be a patient showing up for a procedure and his case not being in office for delivery. No excuse! *No excuse*, I say, to have this happen. With a system of checks and balances in place, cases should be in from the lab two days prior to said appointment, preventing a patient from taking off work only to come in and have to be rescheduled. In the event that the case was not logged-in the day before, team members were required to be in contact with the lab and notify the patient in advance, thus allowing patients to have better use of their time.

No matter how many times you stressed this policy, somehow it happened again. You think "Come on people you know this!!!"

When a team member commits this error, as the owner, you hold full responsibility. Scenarios such as this are unprofessional and reflect poorly on the office. To add insult to injury, the entire day is filled with similar snafus. Your thoughts are vibrating some serious non-positive vibes and attracting more of the same. You long for the end of the day and actually contemplate physically positioning yourself on the opposite side of the bed when you retire for the evening. Tomorrow will be a brighter day.

On the flip side—and without physically switching the side of the mattress you snooze on—you can just as easily arise to the perfect day. Waking up feeling refreshed and energized, humming along to the radio, you smile as you easily maneuver amongst light traffic on your morning commute. The sun shines in all its glory. You arrive at work and learn during morning huddle that many of your favorite and pleasant patients are scheduled. Delivering beautiful cases with textbook-perfect fits and precision requiring no adjustments, the whole team is on point all day and your patients are gracious. You have a warm sense of fulfillment. Ahhhh life is good! You love your job!

We all have a day, every now and then, that may be a little off. And, on the rare occasions we experience Murphy's Law, we must focus on that which is good! In turn, we will receive more good!

28

It's Hard Work!

Dentistry is hard work physically and emotionally; plain, hard work. While attending a continuing education course, I overheard a couple of my colleagues talking about their offices. "It's a freaking zoo," said Dr. Whine, "a mad house." Dr. Whine went on to say he employs three hygienists scheduled full to capacity and he sees a "whole bunch of patients" every day. And with fourteen women working with him, day in and day out, one of them would have something going on either at home or at work, etc. The other dentist, Dr. CEO, chimed in "Yep. You are the CEO buddy... they didn't tell you that in dental school."

It doesn't have to be that way! Let's face it, dentistry is hard work and while you can't get totally around that, you can be more efficient at it by working smarter but not necessarily harder than you already are. Of course, I had to voice my opinion to Dr. Whine and Dr. CEO as they lamented away their woes, "You know it doesn't have to be that way. I am entering the practice management arena and you really can have a team that works hard and is well trained." Dr. Whine replied, "Yeah, I've hired consultants before, but while we are here to see patients, I do want to make money." He said, "You just have to bust your butt to make enough, while each staff member you get is so incredibly bad it is impossible to train them to be good." I countered that he needed to do a better job hiring more qualified team members. Realizing that my words were falling on deaf ears, I listened quietly.

Anything worth having is hard work. I honestly know that there is a better way.

29

Dealing With Staff Issues

Staff issues may involve a range of things: staff members who do not get along; staff members who are difficult to manage; staff members who bring their personal issues to work; staff members who are rude to patients; staff members who are rude or disrespectful to doctors; staff members who don't take constructive criticism well; staff who are not receptive to change; staff members who gossip; staff members who are there to do the minimum and collect a check; staff members who are stuck in their old ways of doing things; staff members who are lazy; and, most of all, staff members who are non-appreciative. Over the years there have been several instances where I have dealt with things I would much rather not.

As a business owner, and a person who deals with the public, you will invariably come across one—if not many—of the aforementioned personality types. What I suggest is to select employees *very* carefully. I have been known to be a no nonsense person, I have an extremely low tolerance for foolishness and simply do not allow it. There is a place and time for everything, and when we come to work it is neither the time nor the place for any of the "staff members" I listed above. We work in a professional environment and should all conduct ourselves in said manner. I used the word staff above because those were "staff" actions. The goal is not to have "staff," but rather a team!

Set the tone for your office and make it clear from the start that personal issues, rudeness, complacency, gossiping, laziness, slackers, and an employee being non-appreciative will equate to dismissal.

30

Large Teams

I had the wonderful experience of working in numerous offices upon completion of my residency. However, I didn't consider it wonderful at the time. Don't get me wrong, I really enjoyed working in most of the practices, but the hours were overwhelming. Through those offices I observed the flow, systems and lack thereof. Some offices had large teams and often the more people employed, the less work got done.

I never wanted an environment with lots of employees. Personalities—several distinct types—are encountered once you begin dealing with numerous team members. Less personalities equates to a decrease in conflict. When I first opened my practice, I was advised that when the office started making a certain dollar amount, I would need to add another front desk person. That concept did not gel with me. I thought it much wiser to hire employees with foreseeable potential (and train them well) and acquire programs/systems such as electronic billing and claims submission that *decreased* the need for more people. There are extremely successful practices operating with few employees. It is much better to have fewer, highly efficient people than a huge team with only a couple of people carrying the load. Not to mention, the impact this has on overhead.

31

Temp Employees

There will always be instances where a team member is ill and out, and this can wreak havoc on a small businesses. At such times one might contact a temporary employment agency that will contract out a person at the spur of the moment for daily employment. Sounds pretty straight forward, right? ...Ah, no!

You have no idea what you are going to get! I clearly remember a "highly recommended" person sent to work the front desk at my practice that had not the first clue about being in a dental office! She had never seen dental software and she couldn't *type*. For the life of me, I struggle to understand why any agency would send a person to work front office—a highly responsible position—with absolutely no clerical skills. Did they not understand that rather than helping us while understaffed it would impose a hindrance on our performance and day?

Cautionary temp tales do not stop there, oh no! I have experienced temps unable to use our high tech equipment resulting in my team stopping countless times to try and teach them, only slowing us down. Temps have been known to break expensive equipment, and some do not even show up! Could this be the reason they are temps? All this is for a rather pricey fee... plus the additional costs to your office due to breakages, time wasted and time lost.

Now do not get me wrong, this is not all encompassing. People are different with different situations and I am certain there are good employees temping for a variety of reasons. I myself temped following my residency and after being an employer, I understand why every place I temped at requested me back.

Sometimes it can be easier to function with the vacant position. I have found that three efficient people do a better job than four, especially when the fourth only serves to throw off the methodology and rhythm of the office.

32

Embezzlement

Horror stories abound about dentists who have been embezzled by "trusted" team members. Usually discovered by the dentist years after the fact, the theft occurs in very small, incremental amounts that become difficult to trace and are barely missed. Upon discovery, the guilty culprit is usually let go and ordered to pay back funds with no charges pressed. It is more of a blow to the employer that someone they trusted would violate them in such a way.

Unfortunately, it is very easy to become a victim of embezzlement in the private practice sector as we often have someone who works upfront alone. If you are with patients all day, it is impossible to know what is going on upfront with the person handling your money. No one wants to believe that his or her sweet team member would steal, but no matter how nice your team members you must take proper precautions. Upon hiring, perform thorough background checks and verify references, and include random drug testing as part of your hiring process. Know your software system back and forth. Run daily reports showing deposits, accounts receivable and receipt data for each day. You may even want to take your own deposits to the bank, but most importantly, *sign your own checks*. By taking these precautions, you can decrease the chances that your company will be a victim of this fraudulent act.

33

Complacency

The whole is greater than the sum of its parts. ~ Aristotle.

Some people get stuck and begin to justify being stuck, while others simply get bogged down in minutia. My advice, observe the law of attraction: If you are positive, that is what you receive; if you are negative, that is also what you receive. Allow me to share a story...

After I had been practicing for about nine years I began taking numerous vacations, one week each quarter to be exact. Whenever I was off, my team was off. Usually they would have the entire week off, but if not the entire week, at least five consecutive days (three weekdays and two weekend days). On this particular occasion, they had a little over a week off and when we returned from this long vacation my first day seeing patients was scheduled for Wednesday, allowing the team Monday and Tuesday to fill the schedule (i.e. move any patients forward to close holes on the book). To my surprise, the book was empty upon my return Wednesday. It was December, and December had historically been one of my busiest months since launching my private practice. At first glance, one could look at the books and be led to believe that patients weren't scheduling. Of course, I didn't buy that, knowing very well that an empty schedule is usually a manifestation of a breakdown in the office system. Immediately I began strategically viewing the schedule, firing instant messages to my front desk person instructing her which patients to move forward and where to place them on the schedule and inviting patients on the hygiene schedule back to have overdue treatments rendered. By the end of Wednesday, Thursday's book was filled and Friday's book was well on its way.

Each day we closed our office with a wrap up of events, and on this day we recanted all of the things that happened in our usual positive manner – and they were numerous given the books were now filled with productive procedures. Then my office administer said one little thing with an air of nonchalance that made me feel like Lou Ferrigno (for those who don't know, he played the Incredible Hulk in the late 70's TV show), "Dr. Teague, when you look at Friday morning don't panic." Now I am generally a mild mannered person, but this comment inspired an out-of-body experience: I felt myself floating straight over and choking her! She obviously felt it was okay to have openings/vacancies on the schedule, and I addressed my views on that attitude in the huddle immediately, and once again the following morning.

I do not advocate operating in a state of panic, BUT, if our last cycle was lower than usual, and we had just been on vacation for over a week, and the office team had two full days to work on the schedule, and the schedule was not filled until I got back and initiated it... *Houston, we have a problem.* The team had reached a point of complacency. After all, they are on salary and get paid no matter how well the office does. My office administrator should have been working with a sense of urgency, not an attitude of "Oh well, nothing is there yet." It is not the responsibility of the doctor to move patients or figure and meet the production goals of the day.

Treat team members like partners in the practice; share numbers with them in an effort to allow them to be compensated as much as they like (bonus incentives); but when the self-motivation of the team is not there and they become relaxed, the perks may have to be removed. Do not reward mediocrity or complacency.

34

Mediocrity

Mediocrity can show its, well, mediocre face in many different ways. One may think, what's wrong with average? It beats being bad, right? *Wrong!* So-so is simply not good enough. In my opinion, there is something extremely wrong with not doing your best, settling for average, or, being a slacker. It disturbs me to the core.

If you graduated dental school, chances are you are a meticulous, perfectionist, control freak! Don't take offense! I fall into that category as well. Some of us are "worse" than others, but you would not have been accepted in the first place—and you definitely would not have completed the highly intense program—if you did not possess those characteristics. What we control freaks must realize is that not all people think as we do. Exercise tolerance with different people and personality styles, and do not expect everyone to deliver with the level of detail that someone with our background would. We are cut from a different fabric.

However, this does not mean you should accept mediocrity. Surround yourself only with people who do their best within their capabilities. Many a colleague has shared the experience of hearing that little voice or sinking feeling inside that tells them it is time for a team member to go. In most cases the writing is on the wall, yet they try to convince themselves otherwise. You should not operate on emotional justifications such as, "But they are not so bad" … or, "They are a little lazy, but a nice person". Nice won't get the job done. Let. Them. Go.

By allowing an inept individual to benefit alongside hard working A+

employees, you are rewarding mediocrity; in essence, doing a disservice to all – you, the other team members, your patients, and the misfit.

35

Firing

Ah, the delicate subject of giving somebody the proverbial boot! Donald Trump has built a second career squinting his eyes, pointing a wrinkled finger and shouting, "You're fired!" He even makes it look like fun. I beg to differ.

We usually know when someone needs to go, yet this knowledge does not make the act any easier. Firing is something that is very difficult to execute. The best advice I received was to always do what's best for the office, no matter what. People get caught up in others' stories; it's part of being human. After a person has worked for you–if only for a short period of time–you begin to care about them and their wellbeing. You learn about their family, hobbies, and trials and tribulations in life. Do what's best for the office and do not allow emotions to sway you. The best time to terminate a team member is when the notion crosses your mind that they need to go. You will be inherently surprised at how things run a little smoother once the person is gone, and how much better you feel.

As the business owner, the person who has the most invested in the business and the inherit possessor of all the liability, you must always do what's best for the office. Repeat after me, "No matter what!" Often times we know someone needs to go but will keep them in hope that they will improve or quit. In fact, when hiring a new person we know within a couple of weeks whether or not this is someone we want to represent our practice. It quickly becomes apparent whether someone will learn quickly or require constant supervision, take direction well and show initiative or cover the bare minimum to sustain a position. If you hear that little voice inside whispering, "This doesn't feel right," listen to it. Your instincts are always right. An employee who is not doing their job, but you like them as a person? Do not try to justify and think, "Oh, but she is so sweet or nice" etc. Nice or sweet can run you straight in to the poor house—or the nutty farm—if this person is not doing their job.

Handle the situation, even if it is uncomfortable. It doesn't matter if it is a new hire or someone who has been on your team for years. If he or she is not part of the solution, they are part of the problem. Left unaddressed it could lead to lowering the morale of the team as a whole and then you'll really have problems!

36

Turnover

Turnover happens in business and there is rarely a convenient time for it. Often occurring unexpectedly—an employee quitting or being terminated (it is not always due to negative circumstances, as people get married, have babies, or relocate)—you find yourself with one less employee yet all responsibilities remain. This can be a big issue for a small practice with few employees, and the office cannot close its doors because you are short-staffed!

During times of transition, the owner must maintain a level head and keep the office running as smoothly as possible. The interviewing process must be brought into play, and the interviewing process can be a nightmare – compounded by phones ringing to be answered, patients scheduled, supplies ordered, instruments sterilized, treatments rendered, financials presented, and questions requiring answers, can all make one want to hang a For Sale sign on the door!

Change can be extremely stressful. Eliminate some of the stress and set yourself up for the seamless integration from one employee to the next by having a contingency plan in place. Take the time to hire selectively and avoid the typical knee jerk reaction of hiring too fast – a recipe for disaster that will only result in the whole process being repeated. In the meantime, organization is key: keep a detailed description of each position in a manual, a checklist for procedures and materials, and an itemized list of supplies for drawers, sterilization room, closets and storage. Such preparation will ensure that current employees can pick up the slack and cover while you search for a replacement, and your newly acquired team member will enjoy a smoother transition into his or her role.

Remember, as stressful as turnover and transitions can be, it always gets better. As the old saying goes *"Trouble don't last always."*

37

That's Not My Job

Err... *What?* By design, I always had a small team. Maintaining a strong stance about employing highly efficient people resulted in me only hiring one office administrator, one assistant, and one hygienist, and by golly that's all I needed. The beauty of my concept of a small team is that each person was cross-trained to the maximum his/her position would allow. For example, my hygienist or assistant could also present financial options, verify and handle insurance, schedule appointments with precision, and handle any front office transaction just as effectively as my office administrator. This concept is relatively unheard of in most dental offices as each position is specific to that one post. However, by employing my concept of cross training, I never heard an employee utter the words, "That's not my job".

Each team member helped one another out. If the schedule were slow, the hygienist or assistant would work up front in an effort to catch up on administrative duties. If the back was busy, the front office person would escort and seat the next patient in the treatment room. TEAM WORK!!

It wasn't always like this. Early on in my practice (different team members of course), I ran into the situation where the front office team and clinical team were at odds. The assistant would complain that the office administrator was scheduling too many patients thus not allowing her to keep up on sterilization of her instruments. The front office would complain about the assistant. Neither area was volunteering to help one another. So, I launched a project where each person had to work in each other's position. I had this switch in place for one month and each team member had a chance to walk in the other's shoes. Thus began a clear shift in attitude: the whining and complaining was replaced by respect for each other and an appreciation for each employee on staff.

Following this project, I began to cross train each team member upon hiring. The knowledge each team member possessed was accompanied by a healthy respect for one another and teamwork. Systems were smoothly implemented. Patients were always provided with consistent information no matter whom they spoke with because each team member fully understood all areas of the practice. As you can imagine, this also proved productive and most useful during times of turnover.

Consider cross training your employees, eliminate "that's not my job" syndrome and prevent your team members from being "up the creek" in the event that the one person who knows all (i.e. office manager) ever leaves. Ah, sanity *and* efficiency.

38

Hiring

Hiring is a long and drawn-out process. Wanted advertisements must be posted, resumes screened and candidates interviewed. The hiring process is a job in itself. So, in between seeing patients and running a practice, you must perform a superb juggling act and don the hat of human resources, *ta-da!* I know of colleagues who have kept a below average team member only to avoid the inconvenience of the hiring/staffing process.

After combing through all of the non-applicable resumes and plucking out those who actually qualify for the position, one must give the interview. Anybody can give a good interview. So be wary. Do not rush to hire out of desperation. I, for one, have made this dreaded mistake. I did not go through all of my usual channels to screen a candidate properly and can attest, by skipping steps, you end up having to let the person go and start the whole process over again.

Avoid body switch syndrome. Body switch syndrome occurs when the person you interviewed and subsequently hired, is by no means the person who showed up for work! They look like the same person... but the similarities end there. The following steps can aid the hiring process.

During the interview, be sure to ask questions that help you assess the candidate's goals, positivism, and drive. Certain questions cannot be asked such as age, marital status, or if candidate has children, due ethical and discrimination laws. Always verify references and administer personality or other similar performance assessment tests.

Dr. Evelyn Teague Samuel

The ultimate key to selecting a good candidate is the working interview. Many people are extremely gifted at talking a good game; but beyond the gift of gab, they may be highly inefficient. Be certain that a release form is signed for this type of evaluation. One may also consider hiring via temporary employment agencies. Using temporary employees allows one to evaluate work habits and performance, aiding the hiring process and reducing instances of body switch syndrome.

39

Interviewing

Let's face it, anybody can answer a few basic questions, finessing their responses to align with an interviewer's expectations. Unless they are a complete nincompoop! So what do you do when a new hire gives a seemingly outstanding interview but a very different version of that person shows up for work? Aside from cry, "Yikes, I want the person back that I interviewed."

Well, I once had an interviewee show up nicely dressed for her initial interview. She presented well and was scheduled for a second, working interview. Surprisingly, she returned for the working interview dressed like a go-go dancer in an MTV video clip –long psychedelic fingernails, platinum extensions, tight three-quarter length jeans, and an equally tight matching jacket, with open toe sandals. I made her well aware of our conservative atmosphere and conduct at the initial interview, as the majority of my patients were businessmen and women. I don't know what she was thinking… needless to say she didn't get the position.

Also, be very leery of persons hypercritical of previous employers and team members. Study resumes to see if there is a pattern of jumping from one position or job to another. Always do a working interview, check references and have the candidate take a personality test. Ask questions to see if they are a proper fit. Remember doctors, this is your practice, your vision, and anyone who does not see or understand your vision does not deserve to be there.

40

Nobody Cares Like You Care

You took all the risks. You have a vested interest. Nobody will ever care like you care, because it is *Your* office.

Think about it... it makes perfect sense, of course you care more, your office is yours! You respect and value every aspect of it. When we work hard for something, we tend to cherish it. Very different from the child who gets everything they ask for –the parents purchase every new gadget that comes out and they want for nothing. Upon reaching driving age they receive the finest car only to wreck it and expect another one. We see examples like these all the time in our society. On the flipside, you have the rebellious child who hates his parents because they gave him everything. Talk about an oxymoron! The point I am trying to drive home is when you nurture something from its inception, it is natural for you to care more.

While your office may never be as precious to others as it is to you, do not be discouraged. You can find great employees. The key is to hire people who take pride in themselves and their work. Treat your team members like business partners, offer a good bonus system and hire self-motivated, driven people.

41

Attitude

Help wanted! Immediate start. Attractive salary and benefits at our new downtown location for the right candidate. Must be an exemplary team player demonstrating excellent clinical skills and a bad attitude.

Err, not a good idea. Attitude sets the tone for every aspect of your practice or business. I am going to go one step further and state that it shapes all life experiences, interactions, successes, and failures. The way one thinks is instrumental—or detrimental—to what comes their way. But, for now, let's get back to your practice...

When I initially opened my solo practice, I searched for the right team members to inhabit my baby... or, my practice. This was no easy feat. My very first employee was hired to work the front and assist temporarily until we attained more patients and could add more team members. She didn't last very long, as I quickly discovered that she had padded her credentials—incapable of carrying out the simplest tasks, she was completely scattered! Next, I hired an assistant referred by a friend who was selling her practice and moving out of state. I paid for this newly-inherited assistant to go through the hygiene program and she never showed up for work again! *Fool me once shame on you, fool me twice shame on me.* Needless to say, I've never sponsored anyone else through our hygiene program. I hired yet another assistant who was a beautiful girl, but not the sharpest knife in the drawer and left me wondering what institution actually gave her a degree. Then, *BINGO!* I used a temp agency and finally found an assistant who was very good at what she did. However, one of my first thoughts when working with her was, "She is *really* good, but her attitude is AWFUL!" Her abrupt mannerisms came across as very rude; from not speaking to patients when entering the room, to the tone she used when she did speak to them... or to me! Quite frankly, it seemed like she was always mad about something. Initially I attributed this apparent moodiness to being quiet and unexposed, and for some reason, I believed I could change her, inspire her to be better. A word to the wise... you cannot change a pigeon into an eagle; people only change if they want to. She worked for me for three years and ultimately it was her attitude that forced me to let her go.

So what is my point? Simply to possess a positive attitude and surround yourself with team members who think the same. It does no good to attend seminars and receive training on practice management, goal setting, communication and great customer service if your team members are not on board mentally and physically. A "defeatist" mentality, or team member or doctor who feels something is too hard, requires too much effort, or can't be done etc. sets the stage for failure. *"If you think you can or cannot, either way you are correct."* ~ Henry Ford. It is the law of attraction. Dentists, it is your job to set the tone; after all, you get paid the big bucks to be happy or put on a happy front. Look at the bright side of every situation. Post the Attitude poem by Charles Swindoll in the break room or office, and have the entire team review it periodically.

One method that helps to promote a positive air—or attitude—is starting each day with a positive quote. This sets the mood for the day. May I suggest you do the same?

42

Being a Cheerleader

Motivating others at all times, or being a cheerleader, can get a bit old. There are many aspects involved in running a dental practice and daily operations can often feel like an attempt to move Kilimanjaro. When there are new policies to incorporate, new techniques to apply, new materials to become familiarized with, and new patients to woo, the leader—*Doctor*—is expected to be the cheerleader. After all, it's your job to motivate everyone, right? ... Or maybe not!

Let's face it, dentists should always portray optimism even if the sky is falling in – it *is* your practice. We get paid to be a healthcare provider and also to act. I once heard a dentist say he comes in and acts as he is paid the big bucks to always be happy. The jury is still out on that one, as it's only human to have an off day every so often. It is a natural part of life that you won't always be "on", but that doesn't mean that everyone needs to hear about it. Always be as upbeat as possible. If you are always positive, or pretend to be positive all of the time, eventually you will be. If you are always doom and gloom, that's what you will have.

Now this doesn't mean you have to be the "happy pill" for your team members all the time. In regards to motivation, surrounding yourself with self-starter/motivated team members to begin with is key.

43

Discussing Finances

Dentists hate discussing money and often times direct
the patient to the front desk to speak with the office coordinator about the
numbers. Every team member in the office should be perfectly comfortable
talking about costs. However, there are people who feel uncomfortable
discussing finances and simply cannot ask for payment. Such people should
not be working at your front desk. Over the years, I have observed team
members who hear the cost of some treatments and begin to think, "That is a
lot of money!" These team members did not understand exchange (i.e. office
deserves to be paid for services). If a team member feels this way, they can
indirectly convey this to the patient who will pick up on their uncertainty.
There is no shame in offering quality procedures and being compensated
for doing so. Running a business can be very expensive. Running a dental
office can be astronomical! Put simply, it costs to offer services to patients.
Team members have to understand this and be confident, willing and able to
discuss payment options. After all, the patient/consumer pays their salaries,
and if the consumers don't pay for services, it affects the entire office.

When presenting payment options, the team member must speak clearly
and directly. They must never ask the patient, "Do you want to pay?" Nobody
wants to pay! I am sure most people would find something fun they would
prefer to spend their money on as opposed to their oh-so-important health.
Instead they should present payment requests in the following manner:
"Ms. Pay, your cost for services will be $300. Will you be paying with cash,
check, charge, or third party financing (such as CareCredit)?" Allow the

patient to answer. In the event that Ms. Pay says, "Can I just pay $150 and pay the balance at my next visit?" The team member's response should be, "Well, Ms. Pay, we must receive payment either at time of service or time of scheduling (in the event of reserving large blocks on doctor's schedule). We can apply the remaining $150 to a credit card or CareCredit." If Ms. Pay remains insistent on paying only $150, the team member would say, "We would be more than happy to schedule you at a more appropriate time and your payment of $300 will be due at time of service."

If you are in a very nice office, such as ours, it should be expected that quality treatments cost. In fact what business do you know whose services do not cost? In a nice environment, patients don't expect discount patchwork and would not expect to receive this. Our entire office attends numerous courses to be educated on the latest procedures and techniques, and we use the finest labs and materials. Why would we go cheap? Often times when you mention cost to a patient (e.g. cosmetic cases) and you quote them a number, the serious patient has already researched and knows the ball-park price in advance and is expecting to pay that amount. The dentist and team should be able to look the patient directly in the eyes and tell them the numbers. You may be surprised how many patients want the very best and are willing to pay for it.

44

May I Call You...?

May I call you Evelyn? Perhaps this is an issue that only arises with female practitioners, I'm not sure, but I have heard similar complaints from many colleagues.

I have never made a big deal about being a doctor. In fact, on numerous occasions my mother has noted, "You never tell people you are a doctor. You went to school a lot of years for that title." Usually I don't make a big deal of it, allowing it to depend on the setting as to if and when I let people know. However, I am usually taken back when a sales representative schedules an appointment, comes to my very professional office environment, and upon my entering the conference room, says "Hello... May I call you Evelyn?" What does one say to this? Could it be that they are just a bit too comfortable? Is their sense of comfort due to my nice disposition and approachability?

When I was in school, a simple etiquette was taught: refer to men as Mr., and Ms. for women, married or single. Miss and Mrs. were considered sexist due to men not having a separate title due to marital status. The whole point was to never address one by his or her first name unless invited to do so.

Professional women often do not express what we truly think for fear of being considered the B word. The fact remains, when a person has entered your office to make a sale and not had enough respect to refer to you by your proper title, it begs the question as to whether this blatant disrespect would occur with a male counterpart? Each office has its own vibe; some offices are fun and bubbly; mine happened to be very formal, organized and professional. We referred to each patient as Dr., Mr., or Ms. unless otherwise invited. Why wouldn't representatives think it proper to do the same?

Back to the question at hand, "May I call you...?" How do you answer this? You look the person directly in the eye and say, "Well, most people here refer to me as Dr. Teague." *Do not apologize for your title.* After all, you spent an eternity earning it.

45

Dental Jokes

What do you call a dentist in the army?
A DRILL Sergeant!
NOT FUNNY!!!!!!

Okay, so maybe I am the only one, but on numerous occasions I meet someone for the first time and they start telling me lame dental jokes. I don't get it and maybe the expression on my face every single time this happens conveys that. I am sure that you, the reader, can relate, as you are most likely in the dental field. But, just in case you are not, take this little piece of advice... *DON'T.*

DO NOT start off a conversation with a dentist with a bad joke containing bad facts and an equally bad punch line. We really do not think it's funny and most of the time it is nonsensical.

46

Loans, Loans, Loans... and More Loans

Like most, you probably took out loans to fund your education. I come from humble beginnings and didn't have an inheritance, nor did I have parents (who were RICH doctors working in health care – wink!) who could take care of my tuition. So I did it the hard way, by taking out loans. I am not complaining, hard work builds character... and I have a lot of character! I took out loans for dental school and another loan in order to live during my residency. And the largest loan of all, I took out to set up my dental practice.

Depending on the structure of your loan(s), you could be paying them back for a lifetime. The smart thing to do is to not take the longest repayment option. This only prolongs the pain. The debt still has to be paid. If you select a shorter repayment term, the payments will be much higher but you will save sometimes hundreds of thousands long term. And once the debt is paid off, you will begin to see, and perhaps even enjoy, the fruits of your labor.

47

Your Life Just Kinda Passes You By

It took many years to get to where you are. Four years of undergraduate schooling, four years of dental school, and 1 to 3 years— if not more—of extra training via a residency, if you chose a specialty. Meanwhile, your friends have already started their lives. Once you become a doctor and start a practice, you invest many more years building a successful business. In the event that you are not a trust fund baby or your parents didn't contribute numerous donations toward your education, you will have to take out a sh-t-load of loans to start up. Spending countless hours, days... *years*... working to pay off "good debt," before you know it your life will have passed you by and you'll catch yourself wondering whether you gave up your best years, and if so, what it was all for.

Solution? Learn to enjoy life! Don't take everything so seriously! Make time to do things that make you happy and that you enjoy. Take up hobbies. Make a list of things that make you happy and do them. Write it down. Periodically, during my office team meetings, we all write our goals at 6 month, 1-year, and 5-year intervals, listing goals under the different categories. Be specific when recording your goals. At this very minute, I am on a plane to Uganda, Africa and I will be traveling to Paris in a few months... all after writing down my goal to travel on my goal list and giving these travel goals a specific date or timeline during our last goal writing session. Interestingly enough, instead of one destination, I will be checking off two of my dream–and goal—destinations before the date I listed. Writing goals works! Take time off, it's important! If you don't take care of yourself and you are no longer around, guess what? There will be no office!

As you age, things that are important begin to change. At the end of his or her life, no person marvels over how much time they spent working or at the office. But many do reflect on the importance of life experience, family and loved ones. Think about it... what's really most important or valuable to you?

48

Ugh! The Sleepless Nights

I have always been somewhat of a night owl. You know the type, the person who comes to life late at night, the one who will talk your ear off when everybody else is ready to retire. Well, I am just like that—not unlike the child who won't go to sleep for fear of missing out on something—I will grab a computer, a magazine, or watch a TV show, busying myself with anything other than what I should be doing... counting sheep! I can function with very little sleep. But, is that a good thing?

Exacerbated by dental school, a program requiring long hours of study, often until the wee hours of the morning, my night owl syndrome often saw me up all night. Fast forward to being a solo practitioner and small business owner... ugh! The sleepless nights! A combination of night owl syndrome compounded by the inability to turn it off, the minute you lie down your mind is awash in thoughts: *Ms. Irritable is on the schedule tomorrow... Oh goodness, I have a team member out sick, we will be short-staffed... tomorrow will be a zoo. I hope Mr. Impatient's case is in from the lab... Oh no! I have to do payroll tomorrow...* etc. etc. Battling it out in your head, the thoughts compete to take dominance and remain the center of focus. All while you should be getting your most important beauty—or should I say *health?*—rest.

Launching my practice, I started with early hours. My first patient of the day was scheduled at 7:00am. Generally arriving at 6:30am to organize and prepare for the day – ensuring treatment rooms were ready, everything in place, and reviewing the schedule to allow for a smooth flow, we would leave promptly at 4:00pm. Now, staying up very late and waking up very early is not compatible. While I can function with little sleep, I do not *like* waking up in the mornings. It has always been a huge production, the alarm goes off and I mutter some inaudible groan and hit the alarm... snooze... alarm blares... groan, hit the alarm... snooze. This goes on for several rounds before I finally jump out the bed and it's off to the races! Once I am up, I am fine and in good spirits. However, I wake up feeling exhausted. Exhaustion, stemming from thoughts of the day to come, is quickly covered up by a cup of morning Joe upon arrival at the office.

Insomnia can be very, well... tiresome! You have to learn to turn it off. Getting proper rest is VERY important for one's general health and this should not be discounted. Here are a few tips that may help:

- Establish a sleepy time curfew and enforce it upon yourself – if you know you have to get up at five, you should not be up playing Words with Friends, or watching late night talk shows until 1:00 a.m. Try to go to sleep at the same time every night, at first it will be difficult, but eventually you will adapt and begin to fall asleep.

- Eat right and exercise.

- Take a warm hot bath just before going to bed.

- Drink some tea or warm milk.

- Remove the TV and other work items (do not balance the check book!) from the bedroom and shut off the Internet.

- Keep the room dark.

- Keep a note pad by the bed and jot down what is bothering you when it enters your mind. It will be there tomorrow! And remember, many times the thing you worry about in your sleep never comes to pass.

49

Working So Hard

Dentistry is HARD work. If you are someone who has been tenacious your whole life, then you expect to work hard and are accustomed to it. Dental school thoroughly prepares its students for this arduous profession... or does it? Sure you have numerous classes, and the volume of information with which you are saturated is unheard of, but you manage to somehow cope and adjust to the enormity of it all. Taking basic science courses, gross anatomy, histology, and neuroanatomy to name a few, you also have dental-specific courses such as dental anatomy and biomaterials, peppered with lab courses to develop your clinical skills. But what happened to the business courses? Which bright spark left that off the curriculum?

Fast forward from dental school to life in a dental practice, where you find yourself supervising a dental team, managing a patient pool, dealing with insurance companies, marketing, and the list goes on and on. You are the CEO of your own company. Furthermore, you have to provide treatment to patients, which can wear on your body.

All of the time I hear, "If only somebody had told me." Well, I'm telling you now, it is *HARD!* If you are considering a career in dentistry, might I suggest shadowing a dentist to see what it really entails? Do your research first and then there will be no surprises. People often go into careers blindly; the motivating factor could be the notion that a career offers a lot of money or flexibility. Do not get me wrong, dentistry can be a very rewarding career, but as with any other thing in life you should do your homework to make sure that it is something that you will really enjoy.

50

You Always Gotta Bring Your "A" Game

Ah, the illustrious "A" Game. The ultimate, your best, premium, precise, crème de la crème - call it what you like, you gotta bring it!

If you made it through dental school, you are probably acclimated to achieving. Dentists tend to be detail oriented, ambitious, driven, highly intelligent and analytical people... not to mention, decidedly good-looking (wink!). Often diverse, we usually enjoy a multitude of other interests. We may be dentists by profession, but venture into many other professional or artistic areas. We are constantly "bringing it." As the owner of a dental practice one may deal with cyclical moments throughout his career. Once upon a time, a student finished dental school and hung his shingle outside, and just like that patients were there and the rest was history! Dentistry has always been a stable career choice, but what if you want more than stability?

Here is what I suggest: put on your mental fatigues and get mentally tough. Determine what it is you want and visualize these results. Close your eyes and see images of you and whatever success you desire coming to pass. Think about how you will feel when this happens. Many a great athlete practices such mental simulations prior to competing. It is not uncommon for Olympic athletes to run the entire race in their mind before it happens and see themselves upon the podium receiving the gold medal for their country. Come on, you can do it! Let's see your "A" Game. Even when it feels like the odds are against you, or you experience a brief moment of mental fatigue, "You still gotta *bring it*!" Dig deep.

51

Change

I think most would agree that change is difficult and that people usually have a hard time with it. Whether a change in career, personal life or otherwise, entering the realm of the unknown can be quite frightening.

In dentistry the change begins when you first start school. Dental school (as I imagine is the same with other professional schools) is quite different from undergraduate studies. The curriculum is much more in-depth, with a higher volume and longer hours, etc. As one matriculates through the program, it never really becomes less intense, rather the person adapts to the responsibilities and workload.

Then comes graduation where the graduate, and their classmates, are faced with what to do next – a residency, an associateship, or a specialty? What next? I recall that period of not knowing what to do, where to live, how to approach my next phase of life, or even knowing what my worth was. Back then, and even now, it felt like the decision I made would impact my life to a point of no recovery. Experience is the best teacher, and it proved that things work out. They always do! Why then, do we put ourselves through these extremes of gut-wrenching worry?

It is psychological. I opted for a residency to allow more time to figure out my life plan. After that year was complete, I faced the same anxiety of trying to figure life's next step. My next steps were independent contracting, an associateship, and then a solo private practice. Amazing how there always seems to be a way out of *no way*.

In private practice, we are constantly faced with making major changes: when to hire, when to expand, and the list goes on and on. Each phase of dentistry (life!) presents new challenges and each dynamic brings change. Change is good! If our surroundings stayed the same, one would remain stagnant and never grow. Everything in life happens for a reason and concurrently exists, as it should. Stay present and enjoy each moment, using experiences to grow. We have all heard popular expressions such as, *"Don't miss the forest for the trees"* or *"It is the journey and not the attaining of the goal which is most rewarding."* Be positive and do your part. The rest will take care of itself. Remember the mantra: *Change is good!*

52

Enslaved

A high prevalence of dentists share the sentiment of feeling enslaved. I loathe the fact that many of my colleagues feel trapped and yet refuse to look outside of the box. Following my residency, I worked for a temp service as well as in many offices as an independent contractor/associate, thus allowing me to witness this mindset first hand. I discovered that a lot of dentists are afraid to do the kind of dentistry they desire; and while I can testify that the majority of dentists want to provide optimum care for their patients (help them) and create beautiful artwork (teeth!), I found that many are stricken with fear.

Fear that insurance won't cover the premium care diagnosed and recommended, rejection from the patient, and fear that the patients think they're just trying to make money? News flash! You are trying to make money, moron! You are a business owner. You are in business to make money, and if you are not, guess what? ...You won't be in business for long!

While attending a cosmetic seminar, I chatted with colleagues over lunch and one dentist who I immediately felt empathy for stated that he only did fillings. That's it... all day long. He had a huge staff and overhead but he never recommended crowns and the sort because he feared the cost would scare patients off. Talk about enslavement. If you are a dentist, or have worked in a dental office, you know that fillings do not generate much revenue. This poor dentist was rolling from operatory to operatory doing mere patchwork, based on his own assumption that if he offered the necessary work, his patients would abandon him. He was over-staffed, had to be strapped for cash, and was doing a gazillion fillings to meet the overhead. It was impossible that he could be enjoying dentistry under such circumstances. But, *"You don't know what you don't know."*

Dentists need to come to terms with the fact that it is not a bad thing to make money. It is not a bad thing to offer premium services and be paid for them. How would you treat a loved one or family member if they were in your chair? Would you present "cheaper" treatment options so that insurance would cover them? Would you want a big amalgam MODB filling in your own mouth because an insurance company won't cover the inlay that is much better for the long-term health of the tooth? An insurance coder is someone who has (very likely) never stepped foot in a dental school. Why should they dictate the best treatment for you, your loved ones, or your patients? Why are so many dentists still afraid to step outside of the restrictive, proverbial box?

Step out people! Just try it. Walk into that treatment room and let the patient know the best option. Present the treatment plan as if money were no object. Present it as if it were your mouth, or your child's or spouse's. Let the patient decide. Will some leave? Yes, of course. And that is okay. Most patients will not leave you but instead feel confident that his dentist has their best interests in mind. Good health is as priceless as your freedom.

53

Rejection

I dare say most people are afraid of rejection. Many decisions are made—or not made—in life for fear of the unknown or rejection. In the dental practice, there may be hesitance on behalf of the team and the doctor with case presentation. Many a dentist does not express all the options for the mere thought that the patient will object to or reject treatment.

As clinicians, we diagnose. The patient comes in and we perform a thorough exam, view x-rays, and immediately launch into what the patient needs. We are trained to recognize, diagnose, and treat findings to resolve problems or prevent the patient from having problems in the future. But, what about what the patient wants?

Many times after asking patients want-based questions, I have learned about concerns, insecurities, and desires. I recall a patient who had a healthy dentition and no problems per se, but revealed during these questions that he always just wanted to straighten his front few teeth. Turned out that he didn't know there was anything that could be done because no one ever asked him what he wanted. I ended up straightening his teeth with Invisalign. Interestingly enough, many patients don't express areas of concern without being asked.

We have a professional obligation to educate and inform the patient of necessary treatment. However, by posing proper questions, the dentist can also find out what a patient's true concerns and desires are. He may find that the patient will be most receptive to the options available, especially in the event that the patient's concerns can be addressed.

It is always best to present patients with options. If you receive a no (rejection), it may mean no for now but yes to future treatment. I have experienced many patients who come in years after being presented with treatment plan options deciding they were "ready to start treatment." Do not be afraid of rejection.

54

Que? No Siesta?

Being cooped up in the office all day gets old. My office boasted beautiful views from each treatment room and over the years, I fell into the habit of never leaving for lunch. In dentistry, a procedure can easily become more extensive and take longer than anticipated, and the dentist always has to be present in office, i.e. for hygienists to see patients (in state of Alabama). Many people think if you own the business you can be off whenever you want because you are the boss, but the reality is that you must be present more often as you carry the sole responsibility... for everything!

Learn to be more creative with your time. Schedule productively and allot enough time for procedures. Getting out during the day, even a meager one-hour lunch, is important as it keeps one fresh. Use the time to connect with other colleagues, network, or just to catch a second wind to complete the day. Do not underestimate the power of a short break!

55

Knowing a Lot of Things
About a Lot of Things

In dental school, we are trained in all the areas of
dentistry. There are eight recognized specialties in dentistry –Prosthodontics,
Oral and Maxillofacial Surgery, Endodontics, Periodontics, Pediatric
Dentistry, Orthodontics, Radiology, and Oral Pathology. As a specialist, one
concentrates on their respective area of dentistry, i.e. Endodontists do root
canals and this is mainly what they concentrate on. As a general practitioner,
one is performing an array of procedures throughout the day, thus creating
the need to constantly stay on top of all the new developments in all of the
specialties. One may start the day with crown and bridge, then move to
Endo, then Pedo, then surgery, etc. Depending on the schedule, knowing
a lot of things about a lot of things can result in one very tired, worn out
dentist by the end of the day. The beauty of practicing general dentistry is
that you can do what you like to do and NEVER do the procedures that you
don't like. Schedule procedures that you enjoy. If you don't like surgery,
refer it out to a surgeon.

56

Some Cases Will Fail

Even when you do your very best, not all cases will have a favorable outcome. An instructor in dental school often repeated the mantra, "Some cases will fail", and all I could ever think was, "How can that be?" Individuals drawn to dentistry are perfectionists by nature! We deal in mere millimeters—tiny increments—and are extremely detailed (otherwise known as OCD). It is hard to decipher whether we chose this field or it chose us based on the certain personality required to do this for a living. As shocking as this may be, we did not create teeth! The Supreme Being created the intricate dentition that patients often destroy with poor oral hygiene habits and decay etc. What makes us think we can create something that will last longer, or be superior to what God originally gave us? Impossible.

I pride myself on being a meticulous clinician, and I, too, have had some less than ideal cases. When things do not go as planned, it is not necessarily a failure but a learning opportunity; allowing us to be creative, learn, and explore different treatment modalities. If everything always went exactly as planned, there would be no room to grow. Approach each case, especially those that may have a less than ideal outcome, as an opportunity for growth and *you* will never fail.

57

Multitasking

Multitasking is generally viewed as something good. Women are naturally adept at multitasking: taking care of the kids, working, taking care of the home. Another good example would be driving, applying makeup and handling a conference call on the cell phone all at once... but I wouldn't recommend the latter.

We are taught to believe that the more things we can juggle at once, the better we are. This leads to being busy, but not really doing much of anything. Wouldn't it be better if you could focus on one thing, accomplish more and achieve more free time, while ultimately being more productive? Well, guess what? You can!

This is a very simple solution, but a solution it is. Use a checklist! Start each and every day with one. Apply this golden rule throughout your office proceedings as well as with your personal activities and allow this simple pearl of wisdom to keep you on track.

One obvious example of how well checklists work would be in the clinical arena where the many responsibilities and tasks relating to patient treatment see the clinical team constantly multitasking – administering anesthesia on the patient in operatory one and finishing the procedure in operatory two while the patient in operatory one is numbing. However, I dare say that one of the biggest pet peeves for dentists is not having a treatment room completely set up during a procedure. It is very trying to begin a procedure only to have to keep on stopping and starting because everything needed is not in the treatment room. The assistant is constantly getting up to go and get instruments or materials, etc. Not only is it distracting but it also looks unprofessional and prolongs the procedure for the patient. Have your assistant draft a checklist for everything he or she needs for each procedure. The room should be routinely set up using the checklist, decreasing the need to multitask while facilitating productivity. Ah, checklist bliss.

58

It Only Takes One Bad Month

One of the things I love to do is exercise. Love, love, love it! Exercise is like therapy for me. It makes everything all right. The air seems cleaner, and the sky a more brilliant shade of blue, following a good healthy sweat session. We all know that hard work on a fitness regimen can yield impressive results. Not only do you feel better physically and mentally, but you look better too! One can spend hours, days, weeks, and months attaining a fitness goal... only to have a two-week vacation undo it all.

In Dentistry it takes just one bad month. Hours, days, months and years of hard work, excellent service and high production can be brought to a screeching halt by one miserable, bad month! This is a rude awakening. You don't expect to look up and find yourself in a pickle. That's only for slackers, right? It doesn't happen to practitioners who generally excel or are well known to be overachievers.

Well I'm here to tell you. THIS-CAN-BE-YOU. Sometimes you do all you can and all that's left is to just say, "Uncle"! If you are spiritual, this is the time to call on your faith; not all things are within your control. And believe it or not, things always work out for the best. However, you must keep doing what you do well, don't give up and press on.

59

The "Hook Up" Dentist

I received an interesting phone call the other day. One of my colleagues called with a question and the conversation went something like this…

Colleague: *Hey, Evelyn? You remember Dr. Famous, the doctor at the forefront of dentistry with the A-List patient clientele?*

Me: *Sure, I remember Dr. Famous.*

Colleague: *Well, one of Dr. Famous' associates, Dr. Referral, called me yesterday wanting to refer a patient to me. Only, the patient is a friend of Dr. Referral… some kind of fitness guru and apparently a really awesome guy and good patient. Anyway, Dr. Referral wanted my services provided to his friend in exchange for private fitness instruction…. what do you think? Have you bartered with patients before?*

Me: *Err, NO! And I don't understand why Dr. Referral is sending this guy to you if he's such an exemplary patient… or why on earth Dr. Referral would expect someone else to barter services?*

Colleague: *Well, I will only barter 30%… I'd I expect him to pay for the balance of the service. I mean, seriously, fitness instruction? How much could that be worth?*

Me: *Are you serious! Let Dr. Referral take care of his friend!*

Colleague: *Dr. Referral can't, Dr. Famous doesn't allow bartering.*

BINGO!

Why on earth would any doctor barter his services? Dr. Famous would not—*and should not*—allow bartering, so why would you? Especially bartering via referral, with somebody you do not know. You don't want to be known as the "hook up" dentist! This will only serve to attract patients who don't value your services and want deals or something for nothing. I strongly believe in paying for services and receiving payment for services rendered. Paying for services keeps all parties happy. Bartering becomes very complicated, as someone will always come out feeling they received the short end of the stick. It is nearly impossible to exchange exact values, and one party almost always feels like the value of their service was worth more than that which was received, potentially placing strain on a relationship. Not that exchange for services can't work, but proceed with caution.

On one occasion, I went against my better judgment and was to provide a service and receive one in exchange. The service I was to give was a short procedure, and the one I was to receive would require several appointments over an extended period of time. I found, over that extended period of time, that it became harder and harder to receive my promised services. The exchanger was either never available or when available, it was evident that I had become an inconvenience. Over time people forget the agreements they make. This incident reinforced my strong resolve on bartering, but that's just my opinion. Proceed into the murky waters of bartering with extreme caution.

60

Burnout

A quintessential "dictionary" definition of the term burnout would be as follows: *Fatigue, frustration, or apathy resulting from prolonged stress, overwork, or intense activity.*

You should be aware of burnout if you are experiencing symptoms such as a lack of fulfillment, or physical or mental fatigue, or you simply feel like you cannot keep going. The many aspects or channels of dentistry make it easy to reach the point of complete burnout. In fact, some of the leading dentists in our profession reached a similar point at some period in their careers.

One particular story comes to mind about a famous dentist, the founder of one of the leading cosmetic continuums in the world, who experienced burnout. I recall sitting in a conference room attending an extensive advanced training session and listening to him voice some of the same woes I felt. This famous lecturer spoke fervently, stating that after practicing dentistry ten years and getting fed up with the insurance companies' bureaucracy, he was on the verge of seeking out a new career. Instead he pursued his dream of focusing purely on wants-based dentistry and pain control. Of course this was not done without opposition, but it was achieved and he is now one of the leaders in our profession. Far be it for me to say, but it sounded like he was facing burnout.

I'm not saying that in order to combat burnout you must launch a new institution, or add more projects to your life. If you are bored with dentistry, but there is an inner pull that keeps you at it, you may in fact need a break.

If you are saying, "I need a vacation," you are already overdue and may be experiencing burnout. If you are doing procedures on autopilot, basically going through the motions without much thought, you are experiencing burnout.

Solution? Take some time off or reignite your passion by enrolling in additional courses that are geared toward the type of dentistry you really enjoy doing.

61

Don't Get Paid for Being Sick

Ask me how many days I've taken off in my twelve years of practicing dentistry and I can respond without thinking. The answer is zero. Zilch. Nada. None. No days at all. Comprende?

This perfect attendance record could be due to the fact that practice owners don't get paid for being sick. Does this mean I haven't had a sick day in twelve years? Now, I do stay in pretty good health—thank the Good Lord! —I exercise and try to eat healthy. But, that's not it. I merely haven't had the luxury of relaxing at home and nursing myself back to health. Instead I would go in to work with a sore throat, snotty nose and draining sinuses... I know, gross huh? But, I was at work, and heaven forbid I not be available for patients who have taken time off from their work and scheduled to come to see me.

Now, a lot of this refusal to take off even if I was feeling like I was knocking on death's door was the fear of loss of production and not wanting to inconvenience my patients, but my strong work ethic also played a role. I have the strongest work ethic of anyone I know. I am not bragging, because this is not necessarily a good thing. I remember being in college and on the dance team in the band. The band at an HBCU (historically black college/university) is sacred and we practiced until the wee hours of the morning and had super long band camp sessions in the Alabama summer heat. Growing up, I was severely asthmatic and suffered major attacks until I was in my late 20's, yet I would still go to practice wheezing and unable to breathe. I would go to class so congested that I didn't know if I'd make it. My mom used to tell me, "you need to stay home and go to the doctor", to which I would respond, "but I have a test!" Pure craziness. One time she retorted, "Well you won't be able to take a test if you're not here." Unfortunately that same determination or work ethic carried over into adulthood and while good in many aspects, it can be dangerous for one's health. Note to the wise (and self): Take care of yourself first.

Now after practicing twelve years and learning to adopt the habits of a seasoned vacationer, I know that failing to administer self-care is foolhardy. One day away from the practice does not a practice make (or break!). I am also convinced that patients would much rather come to see you on a day when you are not barking and sniffling over them—even if wearing a mask and gloves! And even though we are at a higher risk of catching things from patients than they are from us.

Point is, while we may not get paid for being out sick, not taking time off to stay healthy may put us at greater risk. Take care of yourself and use sick days if you need them.

62

Exhaustion

Have you ever felt *exhausted*? You are not alone. Dentistry is exhausting and as clinicians we often wind up feeling physically spent. Our profession is most definitely physically demanding, yet the fatigue is more often a direct result of mental activity. Of course we sit in a weird position with our neck bent using a small visual field for up to eight hours a day, resulting in neck, back, and muscle pain. Moving from chair to chair seeing numerous patients throughout the day can also lead to one feeling physically overwhelmed.

And that's just the physical! However, I would like to focus on often-overlooked mental strain. When we constantly notice we are feeling tired, the majority of this sensation arises from mental exhaustion. One may be treating a patient while mentally working on solving the many issues that arise on a given day, such as daily operations and fires needing to be put out, which all keep the mind constantly working. If the dentist is mentally exhausted, it is not humanly possible for them to be productive.

Design time away from the office to recharge your battery. Time away does not mean staying away from the office but logging on by remote computer access! Time away means true time off, as in, there is *no work being done*. Taking time off mentally and incorporating self-care such as regular massage therapy can ease the mental and physical demands of the profession.

63

Overwhelmed

Do you ever get the feeling that this whole dentistry thing is overrated? You went to school for a hundred years and it's just not paying off. In debt up to your eyeballs, you have invested and invested in this career, yet you are still not reaping the fruits of your labor? Are you bogged down with all the daily responsibilities that come with being a clinician *and* an entrepreneur? Due to all of the schooling, do you feel like you started your life late and are still trying to catch up? Does everyone in the office come to you for *everything*? Does it seem like your team members don't quite understand that while you are there to provide health service, you must acquire a monetary exchange in order to stay in business? Does it feel like you have to beg patients to have services that are solely for their benefit and (not to mention) important for them to stay healthy? If you've felt any of these things, chances are you are overwhelmed… And I thought it was just me who felt this way.

During one of my many continuing education courses, I was introduced to an old concept that was new to me at the time. Little did I know that, if applied correctly, this phenomenon would prove to be a solution to the sense of feeling overburdened. The very well-known key speaker at this course spoke of an Italian economist, Vilfredo Pareto and his concept, which has come to be known as "Pareto Principle" or "Pareto's Law". The economist's concept spurned from observations he made in his garden. That's right, his garden! Where twenty percent of his peapod crop yielded 80 % of his pea production, applying his theory to his work, he noted the distribution of wealth in society – once again, 80% of the wealth was produced by 20% of the population. Pareto's law has come to be known as the 80:20 rule and is reflected in outputs and inputs all around. Each and every person in the room had an "ah-ha moment"! After this brief introduction, I researched and read books containing this law.

Let me demonstrate this concept that has been around for many years as it applies to your dental office:

80% of your headaches come from 20 % of your patients

80% of your profits come from 20 % of your patients

80% of your office desired results come from 20% of your efforts

How does this keep one from feeling overwhelmed? If twenty percent of your patients give you eighty percent of your headaches, reevaluate whether it is worth holding on to the troublesome few. For example, avoid constantly calling patients who break appointments "to get them scheduled for re-care." Instead, contact the twenty percent who provide eighty percent of your positive yield and who show up for their appointments, pay their bills on time, and respect your office team and policies. Apply this concept throughout, addressing any area that has you feeling overwhelmed.

64

You Never Catch Up

A colleague recently vented to me, "I have so much to do. I am consumed by work... my whole life revolves around it! When people me meet me, they say 'oh, you're the dentist' –is that all that I am known for? I don't want to be defined by dentistry! If only I could catch up and live like a *normal* person." Nodding along as she expressed her frustration, all I could think was, "Wow, this feels like déjà vu!" Each thought she shared had run through my own mind at some point. She was speaking my language... singing my song. Many colleagues share these frustrations or sentiments, there are so many things to do that you never feel caught up.

Listen very carefully, I am either the bearer of bad news, or the voice of enlightenment... the truth is, *you NEVER catch up!* There will always be something you can work on, improve, or research. Lighten up! There is no sense in working yourself to death! Obviously, that doesn't mean you let things run amuck, you must stay on top of your daily operations. But you cannot let the need to perfectly "catch up" drive you to an early grave. There will always be things you need to do, and accepting that fact will see you on the right side of the very fine sanity line.

65

Stress

What exactly is stress? Somewhat an ambiguous term, with meanings that can be abstract as well as concrete, we have come to accept stress as an all too common word with excessive yet warranted use in our daily lives. The ramifications of stress may evoke mental, physical, emotional, cognitive and behavioral symptoms. Many lives are filled with stress! Our daily interactions are filled to capacity with work and compounded by one activity, membership and event after another. Everyone is in a hurry. Life is rushed.

Kids have alarmingly packed schedules these days. Many have a litany of extracurricular activities including numerous sports, musical instruments, and languages to name a few. It is not uncommon for little Johnny to rush from school, on to one practice, then to another. Pressure to exceed and succeed is piled on us from a very early age.

We are all stressed! When people talk about their professions, many lead with "it's so stressful", as if each person feels that their chosen area of expertise is hands-down, more involved than any other. Countless surveys list the top "most stressful jobs." Kids are stressed. Our pets are stressed (go figure…what does Fido have to be stressed about other than his annual trip to the vet or where his next bowl of kibble is coming from?). The United States is known as the most abundant and powerful country in the world. Why, then, are so many Americans depressed and stressed?

There are many stressors in the dental office - invoices, overhead, daily operations, patient issues, etc. which I have made reference to in other chapters ,and I have colleagues sharing symptoms such as migraines and anxiety attacks over these stressors. One must find ways to combat, or preferably, balance the rush of a dental practice and the world. Take time to *stop and smell the roses.* Make time to partake in activities that bring you joy. Life is a gift! And, it is short. Appreciate, maximize, and enjoy it!

66

Nobody Understands

If you are not in it, you simply cannot understand it. Family members, friends, etc. can never fully relate because they are not going through it, or experiencing what you are. No matter how you try to explain the work-related frustrations and stressors, people around you have no idea how much is involved in dentistry and being a business owner (especially a solo practice).

I once read an article written by a dentist expressing how he felt being a solo practitioner. Eloquently written, the author did an outstanding job bringing to mind the feelings we all experience. He correctly expressed that his spouse—and in fact, no one—could ever understand. Of course, I can't recall which journal that was in, but my point is other dentists can relate. Colleagues often confide in me about the daily obstacles they experience.

Talking to other colleagues is a GOOD thing, as they may share similar experiences. Starting your own peer or support group, or even a study club, is a great way to exchange information and support peers within the profession. Creating a positive environment to ward off the feelings of isolation and offering an avenue to discuss cases and learn different approaches and perspectives. Sounds like a win-win to me.

67

Loneliness

The isolation one feels when they are a business owner can be difficult to express. Being a solo practitioner can isolate you to the point where you feel like a lone soul stranded on a deserted island. Add to this equation being a solo, practicing *dentist*. Complicate the equation further by factoring-in a person with personality traits of being a perfectionist and meticulous beyond reason. Trained to the millimeter, this is a clinician who knows every single line and groove on each tooth, one who is extremely well versed in head and neck anatomy and can see the slightest variance from perfect. Do you know how small and finite those tiny grooves and line angles are? This is a person, who would stay up for 24 hours, *wax up a tooth, carve and re-carve, and incessantly couldn't stop until it was—and here's that word again—*perfect*.

Add to this the pressures of handling everything yourself, the insurmountable debt, and the mere fact that you have put so much time, money and education into a career that is showing a disproportionate return on investment. There is no one to talk to... no one who understands... you find yourself in a dark and lonely place. Sure, you have family and friends, but they all think the fact that you went to school and have "doctor" in front of your name means you are inherently wealthy. And we all know that inherently wealthy people live happily ever after.

In dental school we attended lectures warning us of dentists and suicide rates as well as drug and alcohol addiction. At the time, none of us could understand why we had these dark presentations. Upon entering the world of private practice, it became clear why someone might take this drastic approach. This is a very serious subject. Writing this chapter, I received a call informing me that a colleague had ended his life all too soon. The unfortunate reality is that I can clearly see and understand how he reached that point. Loneliness and depression may have gotten a grip on him in a weak moment, and without anyone to talk to, he ended it. We dentists are an interesting group and many of us put on a front and won't talk about how things really are. There are a few of us who are honest and admit—even when we are doing quite well—that we are not perfect and it is not easy.

I can attest to experiencing weak moments; I recall a period of feeling so down, distraught, overworked, and yes, depressed, that I would drive home in my car crying uncontrollably. Crazy thoughts flooded my head. The tiny difference between my colleague and me is that I talk about things. Having an outlet, or someone to talk to, makes all the difference in the world. There is a fine line between sanity and insanity, and it is very normal for people to have weak moments. If and when these moments occur, *please* reach out and seek support systems, therapy and/or counseling. This is serious people.

Waxing of teeth is a technique used in dental morphology class whereby a student uses wax and builds a tooth to scale, in an effort to learn accurate anatomy.

68

Unsolicited Advice

Do you ever receive unsolicited advice? It is okay to receive constructive criticism, that is of course, if it *is* constructive *and* you are asking for it. But unsolicited advice, such as how to run your business, be a dentist, or even do dentistry... well, consider the source. The kicker is when the person advising you has often never seen the inside of a dental school, nor owned a business. What is it about people who feel like they know everything about everything? What makes them an expert on something you have been trained to do?

Once while at a photo shoot, a photographer commented on one of my billboards, a billboard that had been photographed by someone other than her. She went on and on expressing her dislike for my new photo that was featured on said billboard and critiquing what I wore for the shoot. "You should be wearing a white coat and not a business suit, it makes you look like a stock model," she said. "People need to know you are the doctor and not a model." I do stats on my marketing to track what is effective and that billboard was one of my most effective forms of marketing. It brought in more patients and production in the least amount of time than any other form of advertising utilized. Purposely using a different wardrobe to my advantage, I know it makes me stand out because I do not look like other dentists. Simply put, it works!

Yes, I could have gone through all of this with her, but why bother? Sometimes it's just good to let others feel like they have contributed even if they really haven't. Maintain a strong sense of self and never let others discourage you or put restrictions on your capabilities or horizons.

69

Haters

What is a hater? A hater is someone who cannot stand to
see others get ahead; a person who has something negative to say about
others who accrue success whether monetary, achievement, or happiness.
A hater is that person who is green with envy, never happy for others and
always concerned with the pity party, "Why them and not me?" Putting
others down in an effort to somehow elevate their own spirits, a hater is a
sad, sad, sad being.

The profession of dentistry, not unlike other professions, carries an
unspoken code of not speaking ill of other dentists/professionals. This is not
taught, it should not have to be taught – it is something that you just KNOW.

Despite this obvious unspoken rule, there are many dentists who
break this simple code of ethics. I've heard of dentists telling patients they
should not get treatments recommended by other dentists (e.g. cosmetics,
etc.) because they can do something cheaper that lasts longer. I might note
that Dr. Cheap, in most cases, is not well versed in new technology nor
meets the education requirement for the latest procedure. You can't blame
Dr. Cheap for his ignorance because, "you don't know what you don't
know", but comments or judgments regarding another clinician's work are
a no-no.

In my years practicing dentistry, I never uttered a negative word about
another clinician's work to a patient, and in the event that a patient started
down that road I would quickly steer the conversation in a different direction. If you do not know the situation experienced by the prior clinician—

and if you were not there, it is impossible to know—then you are not at liberty to comment.

Solution? Take the high road. Never stoop to muckraking and always treat your patients to your highest standards, providing optimum care. Leave the haters right where they are... STUCK.

70

Nay Sayers

Don't you hate people who constantly point out why things won't work? They may be patients, team members, friends or family, and they may not be doing this out of spite but rather a different reality. In their minds things may not work, but their reality does not have to be yours. Think big!

I had the pleasure of being a keynote speaker for my Alma mater, Alabama A&M University, for Women's Month a few years ago. I tailored my entire keynote speech around the individual and the people surrounding her. At an early age, I came to realize I had the ability to create my own reality and achieve any goals I set. I also observed that many people discourage fore-thinkers. Unable to compare myself to the greats in history, my relatively "small scale" thoughts were shot down by superiors and instead replaced with reasons why my ideas wouldn't work. Luckily, I didn't listen. Many people are afraid of their own greatness or ability. Don't be one of them.

Wouldn't it be great if young people were encouraged to believe that they really can do anything they set out to do? One of my favorite quotes is, *"The only thing that stands between a man and what he wants from life is often merely the will to try it and the faith to believe that it is possible."*—Richard M. DeVos

71

Nonbelievers

Nonbelievers are people that always believe that you can't. Every man and his dog told me it was a crazy idea to put a practice in downtown Birmingham. Each person I came into contact with during my planning stage told me that it simply would not work, from the small business counselor (who shall remain nameless) to the interior architect!

The Small Business Administration is the one place you should be able to rely on for encouragement and support when embarking on the enormous task of launching a new business, yet I received nothing but discouragement. Each time I met with my assigned counselor I left feeling deflated. This, my friends, is negativity. One day during our meeting he said, "Just because you have a new idea, it doesn't mean it is a good idea." I returned home that evening and wrote in my journal. My pen leapt across the pages as I wrote, "He does not know who I am!".... "He does not know that *everything* I decide to do, I do!" Deciding I would not return—if I had I would never have believed that I could achieve anything!—I began trimming away all negative sources.

Anyone who did not see my vision did not work with me. An equipment specialist voiced how crazy my idea was—snip! —I no longer met with him. Did he really think I would invest hundreds of thousands of dollars with his company if he didn't believe in my vision? I kept searching until I found someone who could see my vision and met a wonderful equipment specialist from a different company who helped me every step of the way in setting up my beautiful modern office. It was everything I envisioned.

Never allow nonbelievers to cast doubt, or cause you to second-guess yourself, instead use them as motivators. Nothing should motivate you more than the person who tells you, "You can't"!

"Have great hopes and dare to go all out for them. Have great dreams and dare to live them."— Dr. Norman Vincent Peal

72

Neck and Back Aches

Ahhhh, Friday! TGIF! Another week has come to an end. A week of seeing patients and dealing with all that owning a dental practice encompasses has come to a delightful close. Despite riding off into the metaphoric "weekend" sunset—far, far away from the office—I carry a persistent, nagging reminder of my work. No, it's not mental, through many—*many*—years of practice, I finally mastered the ability to leave work at work. It goes much deeper than that. Then what, I hear you ask?

My freaking neck and upper back is on *FIRE!!!* Neck and back pain go hand in hand with the dental field. Ironically, as I write this chapter, Dr. Oz is on in the background yammering on about neck and back muscular aches resulting from poor posture. Really? Do ya think? So would hunching over a dental chair all day (eight hours plus) with your neck slightly bent be considered good or bad posture? In the past, dentists actually stood up! Searching the internet, I even found mathematical equations depicting the postural positions of a dentist, but one does not need sine and cosine to figure that extended periods of sitting with your neck slightly bent day after day will result in discomfort, or *PAIN*.

So what do we do about it? Quit dentistry? I don't think so. The best ways to combat the perils of dentistry's weird postural positions are daily exercise and occasional—or better still, *routine*—massage therapy and chiropractics. Setting up your rooms ergonomically will also prove helpful. Exercise is pretty self-explanatory, a key element of self-care and a highly effective preventative for both mental and physical stress. Routine massages and chiropractics will help prevent tension in the muscles while serving to provide mental benefits. Finally, a room set up correctly, with proper ergonomics, may extend your practice years, all while preventing work-related pain or strain.

73

Talking Shop After Hours

Following a long week at the office, the last topic of conversation I want to have is about dentistry. Nonetheless, there is always that person at the grocery store or social function who feels the need to inform me about his last dental appointment, or the crown a dentist told him he needs, or his horrific phobia of the dentist. This would be okay if it stopped there, but it rarely does.

There will always be the one stranger who stretches his mouth with a finger to show you a bothersome tooth, going on and on with a long stream of questions after reaching in to touch a germ infested oral cavity... "What does this mean?"... "Do I need...?" or "What does this cost?" Gently telling him that you really cannot diagnose without x-rays and a thorough examination, you try to break away. Usually he will grab your arm—with the same hand that fondled the germ-infested oral cavity—and continue, "I know but..."

As the years progress, we become more experienced at handling diagnostic ambushes by complete strangers. Early on, we are willing to share our knowledge and keen to build a reputation as being mannerly. The longer one practices, he learns that this is giving away his services. This is unacceptable. We didn't go to school for years to give free services or consultations to every passerby, unless we are providing charitable services or providing community service, to which we voluntarily and happily oblige. It is quite appropriate to pass your card to the offender with a smile and say, "Give my office a call. We will get you in right away for an appointment and consultation." Then suggest they go wash their hands.

74

Being Made Out to Be the Bad Guy

I came up with the theme for this chapter before I even knew I was going to write this book! After attending seminar after seminar and hearing more and more doctor bashing at said seminars, I felt it befitting to address this issue once and for all. The dentist is always made out to be the bad guy. Can he or she be so bad given they are obviously footing the bill and investing in their team members by enrolling them in such courses? Not to mention paying the lecturers' salaries!

Today, I attended another course and experienced the same old, over-played, scare tactic style of lecture. The company and lecturer shall remain nameless, but let's just say it was a review course for my team and me, as I wanted to take a refresher and I'd added some new team members since taking this particular course. The lecturer went on a tirade! Generalizing and insisting that all dentists are S-T-U-P-I-D, suffer psychological issues, and don't get paid for their services, etc. This came as a quite a surprise, given many of my good friends are dentists and none that I know want to work for free.

Are scare tactics or insults really necessary to get people to understand? Could it be that the lecturer himself is the simple-minded imbecile? Does he not possess the ability to articulate intelligently and effectively to get his point across or sell his product (because of course, they are *all* trying to sell something) or offer a proven method to productivity and profitability? Several audience team members thought the commentary was hilarious and I could not help but wonder, if any of the members laughing (a little too loud) had any clue what it takes to run a practice, pay off an extreme amount of debt, and oh yeah pay their as--s! Would they still be laughing?

Scare-tactic lecturers usually lament that the doctor "talks too much", "lacks the ability to sell", "is clueless about business", and "under-appreci-ates the staff." Clearly the speakers are trying to make team members feel validated, but what if this is not the norm of the office? What if the team receives great benefits and perks and the doctor is business savvy? Such lecturing can be dangerous and lead to the team not appreciating their bene-fits.

Don't get me wrong, the lecturer brought up what seemed to be a lot of valid points. The main one being that 95% of dentists never retire debt free—a very depressing statistic, but sadly probable. Statistics cited at this seminar indicated that out of 100 dentists who worked 40 years, only one retired with the ability to maintain the same lifestyle. Further breaking down profit numbers, the illustration showed a dentist who had 100K in education debt (a conservative number these days) producing $550k per annum with 70% overhead and a 33 % tax bracket had a profit margin of $55/hour. Somehow, a mere $13.87/hr was left for the doctor. It seemed like some "fuzzy math" as I couldn't quite deduce exactly how he reached these numbers. Having seen similar formula breakdowns early on in my career, as depressing as these numbers were, I knew they were true for a lot of my colleagues.

So, what is my point? Am I for or against attending seminars? Ignorance is bliss, but knowledge is true power! Learn from each experience in life, even if the one thing you learn is what you *wouldn't* want to use... you've learned something! You gain new insights listening to others (though you may have to shovel through manure to get to it). Continue taking CE (dental Continuing Education) courses. Go forth and seek pearls of wisdom, but as you do so, always remember, the doctor is *not* the bad guy.

75

Confrontation

Not all confrontation is bad. Confrontation can simply be handling a situation that may not be comfortable but necessary. Upon hearing the word confrontation, it is easy to conjure that a *WWE* smack down is about to happen. The problem is that most people do not address matters when they are small; therefore, a misunderstanding may fester and become a large issue. Usually there is miscommunication, a party may not fully understand, or may receive information in the manner that it was not intended. As business owners, it is imperative to take on aspects of your practice face-to-face. If numbers are suffering, systems are not being followed, patients are not having exceptional experiences in your office, and the list goes on... you must handle it. Do not be afraid to hurt feelings, which is sometimes hard to do. We are all human and most of us have experienced that sick feeling in the pit of our bellies when we have had to do something as tough as fire a team member, but this is part of being an owner.

Confrontation is necessary to allow systems to flourish. It doesn't mean that there is any wrongdoing. It doesn't mean you must chastise. It simply means that communication lines are kept open, all aspects of your practice are handled in a timely fashion, and clear expectations are vocalized and enforced. Smack downs can then be left to Golddust and Rey Mysterio while you practice dentistry... no acting or costume required.

76

The Brown Experience

I have three wonderful nephews. My middle nephew, AD, in his innocence as a child referred to African Americans as brown people. One day, when he was about four, he returned home and asked his parents, "Why are there not many brown people at my school?" My sister and brother-in-law, who were somewhat amazed by how early kids notice differences, took some time to explain as well as they could. My nephew attended a prestigious school that not many parents, brown or otherwise, have the privilege of sending their children to. His school was very diverse and the children were exposed to many worldly and cultural experiences, yet little did he know that the Brown Experience would infiltrate his future, and his everyday life. There is no way to make others understand it, unless of course they have experienced it. And if you have experienced it, you know exactly what it is.

The Brown Experience is about being challenged to a greater degree than others based on your outward appearance. The Brown Experience is not being taken seriously upon first encounter, or being stereotyped as a result of affirmative action. It is proving yourself time and time again, while your peers are taken at face value. The Brown Experience is replying, "I am a dentist" when someone asks what you do, only for them to ask three more times, "So, you are a hygienist?", or, "So, you are an assistant?"

The Brown Experience trails sales reps visiting your office and has them speak directly to your subordinate employee (the non-brown subordinate employee, of course) for approval of an order that you made. It manifests as resistance from subordinates who feel they are more knowledgeable – even though they only have a high school diploma and you have at least eight years education on them. It is the constant challenge or edge you feel from subordinates, peers, and patients.... and, believe me, it is exhausting!

Now I must concede, fellow Brown Experience-ers can heavily enhance the Brown Experience! I've experienced patients who felt I owed them a "discount" for gracing me with their presence. Patients coming in for services and giving my front office *h--l*, all in the name of getting something for free. Usually this person wants your services for free while she is driving a Jag, wearing the latest designer clothes and carrying the latest designer "it" purse while crying poor the whole time.

So what do we do about this? Unavoidable circumstances will always arise and not much can be done to change that. Unfortunately, whether it is conscious or subconscious, discrimination exists. Is it unfair? Yes. Is it tiring? You bet. Are we able to use this as a crutch or excuse? NO!! As children, many are taught that they have to be twice as good to be considered equal and three times as good to be considered better, and I can agree with that. Be better! Be Wiser! And in your dental office, have clear systems in place (i.e. firm financial arrangements, etc.) and apply them to *all* patients. Whatever the Brown Experience brings, you must always be better, be wiser, be firm and be strong.

77

Rose-Tinted Glasses

Many patients who happen to be students ask me, "How do you like being a dentist?" Before I even respond, this is usually followed with, "Seems like it would be cool to be a Dentist. You make a lot of money and it is not a stressful job." And, when I look at it from their perspective, it really doesn't look all that bad... luxuriating in a boutique practice decked out with all the bells and whistles such as, digital radiography, intra-oral cameras and plush décor. Warm calming colors blush the interior walls and a stunning, panoramic view of the city skyline combines with aromatherapy diffusers, chenille blankets and soft jazz, invoking a sense of calm. Add to this a scrupulous level of organization ensuring this patient did not wait upon arrival and was checked out at the conclusion of their timely appointment and scheduled for their next appointment with their credit card payment posted to their ledger, all while still sitting in the comfort of an ultra soft leather chair in the treatment room. Ah, yes, peace and serenity. Pure Zen.

The reality is that I spent most days thinking to myself, "This job does not pay me enough to deal with its drama!" And by drama, I mean all the stuff that goes on behind the scenes. Now that statement says a whole heck of a lot given I was the one signing the checks! The Boss... The Big Kahuna... The Head Honcho. Where was I going wrong?

Faced with whether to give an eager student the realistic answer or a saccharin-coated half-truth, I knew that no matter how I felt about dentistry, I had no right to discourage anybody from pursuing their dreams. Sticking to my firm belief of spreading positivism, I would tell them, "It's great I love it!!!" And to some degree this was true –I loved *performing* dentistry. Dentistry is GREAT! And so is honesty... so whenever a young student on the cusp of making life-altering decisions would ask me what I really thought of dentistry, I told them the truth.

When it comes to encouraging the young, potential future dentist, we must first help them nix the rose-tinted glasses and instead offer a road map to realistically guide them and warn of the challenges that may lie ahead. Inspire them by sharing how rewarding it is to help others, solve problems, relieve pain and enhance smiles. Advise them to keep their grades up in school, and participate in many community service activities (entry into dental school is highly competitive, being a well-rounded individual is imperative). Encourage them to shadow a dentist to be certain that they enjoy working in the health care arena while allowing them to experience first-hand what the profession truly involves. And lastly, inform them that dentistry is the easy part, running the business requires a lot more attention.

In the past I have recommended that students consider majoring in business while taking the other science prerequisites for dental school entry, facilitating running a dental practice properly in the event that they wish to own a practice in the future. Most importantly, it is our responsibility to impart that anything worth having requires hard work and determination, by rolling up their sleeves and committing to do the work, they can do it... Just like you did!

78

PITAS

Pain-In-The-Ass patients. Self-explanatory? Read on...

79

"D" Patients

You know what I'm talking about, "C" patients are just what they sound like, *average*, a "D" patient barely passes, and an "F"? ... Well, let's just say they failed and you must fire them as patients immediately! Doctor, how could you say something horrible like that? Well... let me elaborate.

The patient who comes in only when they have a problem is very annoying to say the least. When going over the morning schedule, the whole team learns that Ms. Pita is having a problem again. She is in excruciating pain and only wants to come in at a time when the doctor can complete the whole procedure. The frustrating aspect is that you forewarned this person of all the pain to come; almost every tooth needs some kind of procedure! Would it not have been best to have those problems taken care before they became major procedures?

It never fails that the procedure becomes something extremely involved. A tooth that once needed a simple filling now requires a root canal, build up and crown. A tooth that once needed a root canal, build up and crown is now in need of a surgical extraction and a bridge or implant. Then you must listen to the woes of how much the treatment costs, tempting you to grab the patient and shake them until something clicks inside their head! Do they not realize that simple preventative measures would have prevented this? Do they not realize that it "costs so much" because they didn't do their part? Over the years I have heard patients complain about a $100 filling and not get it done. Only to return a year later when they are hurting (amazing how *real* things become when one is in pain!) and need a procedure well over $1000. All the while he or she is not making the connection to, or taking responsibility for, their lack of action.

What can we do about it? Plenty, I say! You own your practice and you can do whatever tickles your fancy! I've said it before, but I don't know if it hit home: *"You do not have to see every patient that comes in the door!"* Sometimes it is just not worth it. Your practice should be full of "A" patients... "B" patients are good as well... "C" patients are average. It's just like school, with tutoring (educating the patient) and a little drive, anyone can become an "A" student (patient), but they have to want it. If the patient really does not care about their health, there is nothing you can do to change this. Accept it and move on. Of course, you have to do your part as a professional and continue to educate them, but in the case that you are fighting a losing battle, refer outside of your practice.

80

Lack of Responsibility

Patients who do not take responsibility for their teeth and oral problems are irritating. The number of patients who come in presenting a self-inflicted, lifetime of teeth neglect and then get upset with the doctor because something hurts and they have to pay to get it fixed consistently amazes me!

If you are a healthcare professional—I believe the majority of dentists entered this field to help people—this is your opportunity to educate the patient and emphasize the need for oral and general health. Seize it! However, while guiding this person to better health, you must allow him to take ownership for his neglect and the health issues he has brought on. Educate, educate, educate!

81

Lack of Value

Patients who really don't care about their oral health will come for appointments. You will recognize this patient within the first few minutes of conversation. This will be the person who, following diagnosis, will say, "Just pull it!"... Or worse, "Just pull them all." Personally, I am in the business of saving teeth, not "just pulling" them.

Then you will have the patient with periodontal disease, you will explain their diagnosis stressing the link between periodontal disease and other systemic problems such as heart disease and diabetes. You offer a treatment plan and try to get them on the right foot to fight the disease, save their teeth and become healthier. They go through treatment only to return for maintenance appointments with poor oral hygiene and fresh plaque indicating that they haven't been brushing their teeth at all—unless, they've been using the handle end of the toothbrush! Yet all the while they'll swear to you that they brush fifteen times a day.

It is IMPOSSIBLE to influence a person who doesn't care. A good practice is to ask questions and listen intently while interviewing the patient. Place the ball firmly in their court, while giving them the options to getting healthier; you cannot press the issue if they do not care enough to address their own health issues..."*You can lead a horse to water...*"

82

Noncompliance

Come on, you know this patient! It is the patient who comes in following years of neglect and needs a procedure on every tooth in their mouth; the patient who opened beer bottles or finger nail polish bottles and cracked a tooth; the patient you saw over a year ago who had a root canal and was strongly advised a crown would be necessary to protect the compromised tooth from breaking. (Of course, they did not get the crown, but here they are in your office today, their world crashing down, upon learning that the tooth is broken so extensively it must be extracted.) This is the patient who blames you for all of their problems and accepts no responsibility for their own, flat-out NONCOMPLIANCE!

We dentists are pretty detailed people and can get too specific. I pride myself on making procedures clearly understood by the patient without overeducating to the point of confusion or submission. My goal is to make them feel comfortable, answer their questions, and give them a general idea of the procedure and what to expect. However, it really irks me when I go over and over a treatment plan, only to have the patient do the complete opposite!

When they fail to heed the warnings by delaying a procedure, (i.e. crown following a root canal) and are upset and have an emergency and must see me right away. When they are over-demanding and get angry and irate over fees, etc. WHEN IT COULD HAVE BEEN PREVENTED, if only they'd listened! Well, it is enough to make one explode.

Noncompliance, in some capacity, will arise when dealing with the

126

public in general. There is no way to avoid it. Some people will not get it, and others just don't want to. It takes all kinds to make the world go around. As health care providers, we must not give up, as clichéd as it sounds. If we get through to one person and help one person, if just one person hears us, then we have done what we are supposed to do. So, my fellow colleagues, take a deep breath and keep on explaining; educate your patients on proper oral health, stay positive and keep hope alive!

83

Being a Psychiatrist

It's amazing how many people are frightened of visiting the dentist. Even more amazing, the number of people who feel their expression of how much they "hate the dentist" is the first time the dentist has heard such a declaration. If I had a dollar for every time I heard this, I would be very wealthy right now. Now don't get me wrong, I feel sincere compassion for each person who comes in with this very real and understandable fear, a fear that usually stems from a poor childhood experience and paralyzes patients through adulthood. If the occasional fear-struck patient was all we had to deal with, it would be manageable, but the fear is often accompanied with a heavy stream of negative thoughts. For example, "No offense, but I hate coming to the dentist and I know this is going to hurt"... "Are you going to shoot me in my gums? I hate shots"... "I know this will ruin my whole day"... "I hate that I have to go to work after this" ... "This is just bad"... "This costs too much"... "Do I really have to have this procedure done? Can't I just reschedule?"

It does not stop there, once the negativity train gains momentum, the patient will begin to vent about all of the other things going wrong in their lives. Negativity is both contagious and draining. Have you ever noticed, after being around a "negative Nellie" (who only sees the dark side of every-thing), that the energy has been zapped completely out of you? Often times, the patient is unaware that they are being negative and will continue down this road of complaining, unwittingly prolonging the inevitable and drag-ging out the appointment.

Over time this can pose frustration to the doctor and team. It usually takes a great deal of time to make these patients feel comfortable, and of course it is important to keep on schedule and not keep others waiting. Psychiatry is not what you signed up for. You have allotted time for a dental procedure and a "session" in your chair is not part of the scheduled appointment.

Employ my tactics and promote an environment of relaxation and positive energy. Encourage patients by telling them "positive thoughts now, no negativity". Say this in a very upbeat, positive tone and use affirmative statements to counter their negative ones. Not in a condescending attempt to minimize their fear, but an attempt to steer them toward a more positive stream of thought. Distraction techniques utilized in my practice also proved to sooth the anxious patient by taking their mind off of fear: head phones; asking them to close their eyes so that light won't be in them; not allowing them to see the syringe; and administering anesthesia *slowly* to minimize any discomfort.

I always make it my ultimate responsibility to convey the genuine care that I have for the frightened patient by taking the time to make them feel comfortable and listening as they express their concerns. Identifying with the patients, I use terms such as "I understand" and take care to select user-friendly terms in my responses and explanations to help make the patient relax. Staying away from terms like shot, pain, and needle, I instead use language such as "discomfort" or, "putting the area to sleep," etc. Patients respond to these techniques and *they relax*. The majority of patients won't even require nitrous and often times fall asleep during procedures. Many patients leave feeling that the experience "wasn't so bad after all" and are much more comfortable at future appointments.

Another suggestion is to invest in a communication course. Years ago, I took my entire team on a two-day communication skills retreat, where they learned how to read patients and identify with them. Many of the techniques learned were successfully employed in our office, smoothly guiding patients from the negative to the positive, facilitating happiness and cooperation from the once fear stricken. When fears are successfully alleviated, many of these people end up becoming the best ("A") patients.

84

Bullies

Okay, so I hate bullies. Doesn't everyone? Bullies are the patients who march into your practice and tell front office staff when they will be seen and how and when they elect to pay for their account. Of course nothing the front desk person says is feasible or acceptable, and of course, they can never come in when you have availabilities on your schedule. They huff and puff and demand and push until they get their way... and guess what? They are still unhappy! Once they get their way, the stage has been set and they will dictate and set your schedule for the duration of their lives visiting your practice.

Here is what I say to the proverbial bully patient, NO! Flat out no. Train your front office that *"no"* really does mean *"no"*. No does not mean, "No, but you can push me until you get a yes". It is important for your office team to understand the value of your time. It is also important for them to comprehend that patients cannot dictate the office schedule. How can that possibly work? How can your office work around one thousand different schedules? And, just what will happen if the front desk person says no? The bully will either accept the terms of the office or go somewhere else, and if they go somewhere else, so what? It would be better for the practice anyway. The office does not need someone there who is so difficult to deal with that it drains the energy of the practice. I don't know about you, but I didn't go to school for years, borrow a gazillion dollars to set up a practice (complete with astronomical overhead) to have some bully come in and tell me when and what to do in MY practice.

Now I say all these things with a hint of jest, but bullying is a serious problem as is reflected in our society today. Many young people have taken their lives over being bullied. Children who are bullies often grow up to be adult bullies, and they are very crafty at selecting their victims. If the person who answers the phone is timid, the aggressor will take advantage of the situation. It is important that your office team understands that it is okay to say no to the bully. The dental team member must remain professional, but firm; often times when people stand up to the nemesis, the harmful acts come to an end.

85

Tardiness

One of the best features of my office is that I run on time and I respect my patients' time. We live in a world where most people are very busy and have to fit a number of things into a short period of time. Practicing dentistry is very different from going to see the physician. A procedure is done at appointments that may require large blocks of time; therefore, not as many patients can be seen during the course of the day. Many times when a dental practice runs behind, it is due to improper scheduling (scheduling too many procedures, thus not allowing enough time for the clinical team to complete treatment), unscheduled emergency patients, and, the most common reason, patients who show up late for their appointments.

Focusing on patients who are tardy, or late for scheduled appointments, I have one golden rule: do not see patients who are late. It is much better to make one apology to the late person that you will not see them, than to have to make several, as seeing the late patient will set a domino effect into motion and the office will undoubtedly run late the entire day. Will the person who is late have a problem with this? Perhaps. But by accommodating the late person, you are in essence sending a message that this is acceptable behavior. This patient will most likely continue to show up late for future appointments, causing others to wait. It is unfair to make one patient wait because another couldn't make it to his appointment on time.

A way to properly handle this common situation is to give patients a courtesy call ten minutes after their scheduled treatment time. A typical call would go as follows:

"Good morning Ms. Late, this is Sue calling from Dr. Teague's office. It is 9:10 and you had an appointment scheduled with us as 9:00 a.m. I wanted to make sure that everything is okay."

"Yes, I know I am parking my car right now," or, "Yes, I am running a little late I can be there in another fifteen minutes."

In the first scenario, depending on the procedure, there would be time to go ahead get the patient in and treated. In the second scenario, the office representative would need to go ahead and have the patient reschedule.

"Well, okay, Ms. Late why don't we go ahead and get you rescheduled? The procedure the doctor has you scheduled for will take a full hour and we want to make sure that we don't rush your appointment. We want to give you the quality service that you deserve. I have a 9:00 a.m. appointment tomorrow, would that be more convenient for you?" In everything you do, always point out the benefits to the patient.

While we can never change the fact that people will be tardy, forgetful, or plain inconsiderate, there is one way around the tardy patient. DO NOT SEE A PATIENT WHO IS LATE. This simple rule will ensure that there is one less stressor to deal with during your day.

86

The God Syndrome

Patients should always be made to feel special. Countless surveys reveal the general consensus of exceptional customer service to be: no one patient is more important than another because every patient is a VIP. From the moment a person enters the practice they should feel welcome, being referred to by their proper name and being seated and treated on time. Patients should also be notified immediately of any delays so as not to waste their precious time. One way to ensure the practice runs on time, which was addressed in chapter eighty-five, is by not seeing patients who are late. Never make other patients wait because another patient showed up late. I was very firm about this in my practice...

My office saw a lot of professionals and often the bigger the title, the bigger the, err, *syndrome*. Egos - super inflated ones! One time, our office team was scheduled to fly out to the west coast for extensive continuing education courses; we had patients scheduled for a half day in the morning, as we were to fly out late afternoon. While we had allowed plenty of time, we needed our day to run as expeditiously as possible and since we ran pretty much on time daily, there was no foreseen problem to our planning … or so we thought.

Our first patient, a physician showed up about twenty minutes late. Scheduled for hygiene and then on my book for an implant, my front desk person informed him that while we could still see him, we wouldn't be able to complete the treatment due to his late arrival. The patient became very irate, insisting if he couldn't have his entire treatment, he didn't want anything done, before storming out of the office. I called the patient on his cell phone in an attempt to exert damage control –my policy of not seeing late people remained firm, but I wanted to make sure my team had been firm yet courteous. When the patient answered the phone he was indignant, "I am a doctor and I was only fifteen minutes late! I was the first patient of the day so you could've still seen me." Now, mind you, hospital settings differ quite a bit from dental offices. It is not uncommon to visit a physician or hospital and wait hours to be seen; and many times, a nurse speaks with the patient and the doctor only comes in for a few minutes. Dental procedures require the dentist to numb the patient and then sit down and actually perform treatment. Time must be allotted for the patient to become anesthetized *and* for the actual procedure. If a patient shows up twenty minutes late for a scheduled one-hour procedure, the dentist would be forced to rush the procedure. Relaying my concerns for cutting corners in his treatment time to the patient, he stubbornly stood his ground. While expressing gratitude for my calling him personally, he informed me he would not be returning to our office. People often want their own way, and the "God Syndrome" intensifies this characterization, leading certain people to feel that guidelines do not apply to them. This patient, Dr. Tardy, was clearly suffering from this syndrome, telling me how to run my book, with no regard to other patients and their time.

By sticking to our principals that day, we lost an implant... but the very next week another patient called to schedule the completion of her implants; a patient I had referred to a Periodontist to place implants two years prior and she was ready to have them restored. A full maxillary case! The patient came in, received her treatment plan, and paid twenty thousand dollars for her case. An older lady with no special title, she was grateful for the care and respect we provided. The moral of this story is that when one door closes another opens. The case we lost, the tardy physician, was a tenth in production *and* a much more difficult patient to deal with. We ended up with a more productive case and an appreciative patient who respected our office, our policies and her fellow patients.

87

The Patient is Always Right …
Except When They Are *WRONG*!

How many places have you worked and learned the golden rule? No, not the *real* golden rule, but the one that says, *"The customer (patient) is always right"*? I believe we should always cater to our valued patients, but what happens when they are, err let's say... *WRONG*?!

Once, my team pulled me away from a procedure on one patient to deal with the irate mother of a young patient who had barged into our reception unannounced, raising hell.... "Why did your hygienist give my daughter five shots? FIVE! Shouldn't the doctor be working on my daughter, not the hygienist?! Why is she doing YOUR work and why did she need five shots?" In the state of Alabama hygienists are not permitted to give injections, so I was utterly confused by this woman's tirade. "My daughter does not lie... and I want answers NOW!"

Apologizing to the patient I was working on, I stepped away to review the chart notes for this woman's daughter whose grandmother had escorted to a previous appointment. Upon review, I discovered that her last appointment had been for sealants. Sealants are a plastic material used on permanent molars to prevent cavities from developing. The teeth are painted, or conditioned, with an acid etchant material, the sealant is placed and the tooth is cured with a light that sets the sealant. There are absolutely no "shots" involved. My guess was that the little girl saw the delivery syringe carrying the etchant; in essence her daughter did "lie", but not on purpose, and Ms. Irate was, can you say, *WRONG*?!

Explaining the procedure to Ms. Irate, she then shifted her focus to what hygienists could and could not do, "I didn't know *hygienists* are qualified to do sealants." Sigh... There will always be people who have to be right. Hygienists are more than qualified to do a number of procedures, and, this was one of them. I informed her of this fact and then allowed her to watch a video on the sealant process and review her daughter's chart – the hygienist had clearly recorded that she explained the procedure to the grandmother who escorted the child for that particular appointment.

What is the moral of the story? Always take good notes, take the time to educate and inform patients, and, take that old adage and change it to: "The patient is ALWAYS right... until they are *wrong!"*

88

Is This Treatment Really Necessary?

"I don't think this treatment is really necessary." We've all heard this from a patient before. It beckons the response, "I'm sorry I forgot, but which dental school did you graduate from?"

Today I was having one of *those* days... not a bad day per se, but one that left me wondering how I was going to cover all of the expenses; a day that, upon reviewing the bank account and collections, I could only see disproportionate expenses. Despite doing everything right, I still felt like the proverbial rat on a treadmill.

One of my very favorite patients, who had been with me for a number of years, came in today and I entered the room with my usual upbeat greeting, "Hey! How are you?" I asked him about his next business trip, whisking him off to some exotic locale that he will never get to enjoy due to it being for business. He kind of half answered the question before going on the attack, "Is this treatment really necessary? All of my fillings need to be replaced at once and I don't think this needs to done. I do have a hole in the back I can feel, but all of them?"

Patiently I explained, "You have several fillings that have most likely been in your mouth for a long time." He retorted, "They weren't done that long ago!" At this point I would've *loved* to say, "Well, Mr. Know-It-All, I am sorry you had crappy work done!" Instead I told him, "You don't have to have anything done, but you do have fillings that have breaks and cracks in them. This means there is micro-leakage that could cause problems underneath the filling... and cavities!" I offered to take pictures of the teeth showing the areas of concern. He interjected, "I don't have a trained eye." I enlightened Mr. Know-It-All to the fact that he did not need to be trained to see obvious breaks and cracks.

Upon taking the photos the patient could clearly see the large openings in the fillings, along with cracks that ran vertically along several of them. A picture is worth a thousand words… "I guess I do need to get those taken care of." Mr. Know-It-All sheepishly noted. I also took "after" photos to compare with the "before", comparing the broken and cracked fillings with the new consistent ones. I knew the work was beautiful.

The moral of this story is you will always have patients who think that you are rich and that you are practicing extortion, not dentistry. A composite filling is not going to retire you. As a matter of fact, they take up too much time and aren't productive —wouldn't it be great if the patient understood that you will never get rich doing fillings and you are, in fact, only doing them for their health? The need for an intra-oral camera or digital camera is paramount. With visual aids, you are able to have the patient co-diagnose, allowing them to see their problems for themselves.

In the case of Mr. Know-It-All, I was profoundly offended by the insinuation that I would treat a patient just for the hell of it. Instead of letting it pass, I let him know how I felt… just because I am a dentist and ultimately a professional does not mean I will take insults. Nobody should.

89

Selective Amnesia? …
Well, Let Me Help You Remember!

Ever had a situation where you informed a patient in depth about a procedure, showed them educational videos, answered countless questions, and, wait for it… had them sign a document stating they had been presented the options, all to have the patient later say, "You never told me that"? Well, I have—many times—and I deem it *selective amnesia*!

I've dealt with frivolous lawsuits – usually arising from dealings with financial options. In all of my years of practicing (twelve), I had—knock on wood—only two instances of complaint. Ours is a highly litigious society, and the fact that our names are prefaced with Dr., makes us prime targets. Of course, we doctors are all extremely wealthy and can afford to give away free money, right? But I digress...

One instruction I gave to each employee and can offer you as golden advice: Document *everything* that happens as if you are defending yourself in court. It may sound like paranoia, and it is an absolute shame that we have to do this, but it is a must. I cannot stress how important this one piece of advice is.

Of the two aforementioned incidents, the first, patient A, owed me money (yes, that's right, owed *me* money) and the second, patient B had an appliance made that was kept for seven months before she decided she wanted her money back. Patient A had initially sung our praises as I had taken a great amount of time alleviating his dental fears and anxieties; he affirmed that no other dentist or dental office had cared for him like we had. The minute his insurance company didn't honor their portion of a covered procedure, leaving a balance for which the patient was responsible, he started sending threatening letters to the office before filing a fictitious law suit.

Patient B, on the other hand, was difficult from the get go. From the beginning, she wanted a procedure done on the "low, low"... Can you say, *red flag*? Once again, the patient sang our praises throughout treatment, which was altered to a less expensive plan per her request. Ultimately dissatisfied with her decision to go cheap, she became belligerent with my team (which I do not allow) and never returned for follow up appointments for her new appliance – despite our office attempting, several times, to reach her in order to reschedule, and despite our offer to make a new appliance—free of charge—if the present one was not to her liking. Seven months later, she called back asking for a refund. In any other industry, a person would not dare return a customized item, whether it be a car, a tailor-made suit or whatever! Why, then, do patients think they can return used teeth? I had offered to remake the appliance seven months prior, free of charge! Oh how fast patients forget being advised about these things and signing a consent form. My response to this "Let me help you remember."

In both instances, my office kept detailed documentation of all encounters with the patients, from phone conversations to missed appointments, to office treatment, to their abuse of my team. And, because my office keeps such detailed information, both complaints were thrown out of court and the patients were ordered to pay my costs for, in essence, *wasting my time*! Prior to fighting this, most people advised me to pay them to go away, but to me it was a matter of principle. If you ever find yourself in a similar situation it is ultimately up to you how you choose to handle it; however, keeping detailed notes will protect you in the event that you are targeted as a get-rich-quick project for an opportunist.

90

I Guess I Just Bought You a New Car

If only I could buy a car with the $100 paid for a filling! I don't think there is a dentist out there who hasn't heard something to this tune. "I guess I just paid for your vacation", or, "I guess I am paying for your fancy office", and so on. The truth of the matter is, in most cases, the overhead per hour is much higher than what a simple filling could even begin to cover.

As far as the, "I paid for your fancy office" comment goes... you wonder if the patient would rather the office be old and dusty with dilapidated equipment, dated technology, and stuck in a bad location? It is often tempting to throw an off-hand statement right back at the perpetrator. I know I want my dentist, as well as any other health care provider, to be up to date on continuing education and technology, have the best team, offer the best services, and yes, have a "fancy office"! Something about dusty, dirty and old, with bad employees would convey the type of treatment I would be receiving. It doesn't pay to go *cheap* with your health.

Don't most people go to work and use the money they make to support their living (i.e. buy a car, pay for home, food, etc.)? Seems straight forward and normal to me... but back to the one single treatment in my office, trust me, you *did not* just pay for my new car!

91

Insurance-Driven Patients

Insurance-driven patients are those who come to the office with a slew of dental problems but only want the work completed that is covered by insurance. Anyone who knows anything about insurance knows that the insurance company will pay the bare minimum for treatment. The sad thing is that many patients come to dental offices, daily, repeating this sentiment. It is very disheartening to hear this day in and day out; we dentists know that what the insurance will cover and the necessary treatment are never the same.

It is mind boggling that the general public willingly allows insurance companies to dictate their treatment. On the one hand, you have a clinician who has gone to school for umpteen years, studied the body and disease process extensively, learned pharmacology, radiology and a number of other "ologies" in order to diagnose and treat patients. On the other hand, you have an insurance coder, usually a person with no medical training, who pays by codes. You do the math... I don't think I would want someone with no medical experience figuring my treatment plan.

So what can be done about this, Doc? The cure for the insurance-driven patient is to educate them about necessary procedures, what insurance does and how it pays. Once educated, the decision is in their hands. I've said it before... *"You can lead a horse to water..."*

92

Patients Misunderstanding What Insurance Is

Countless! I stress, *countless,* patients have shared previous dental experiences and claimed they were told they needed a lot of work done because their former dentist "Knew they had good insurance." Laughable! I've heard it all from, "My insurance is excellent, so I know they were trying to get my money", to my favorite, "Please, do all the work. I am not worried as I have good insurance." We dentists know that there is no such thing. On the other end of the spectrum is the patient presenting a multitude of problems who says, "Only complete the work that my insurance will cover" ... Sigh.

We offer treatment plans to get our patients to ultimate health. Period. Patients are misinformed, and being accustomed to visiting their physician and paying a $20 co-pay only adds to the delusion. There is no way on earth dental treatment can be this way, due to our materials and lab fees alone! Prior to the commencement of any procedures, we give the patient a breakdown and estimate of what insurance will cover.

As for "good" insurance, why-oh-why would a patient believe that a $1000 maximum is "good" insurance? Insurance companies have been offering this amount for at least forty years. You cannot even buy a Coca Cola for what you paid for it forty years ago. Truth be known, "We don't want your *good* insurance." We would *much* rather you pay for your services and cut out the middleman. At the end of the day, the fiendish insurance company reimburses the patient far faster—and often times at a higher rate—than the doctor doing the procedure.

A few years back, I had it up to the wazoo with the insurance companies! Some of their fee schedules, or permitted fees, were lower than my lab fees! Yes, that's right! I was either losing money or doing procedures for free. That's neither right nor good business sense. So, I decided I needed to GET OUT of network for as many insurance companies as possible. When my office began terminating some of the contract provider agreements— or traps—I had a personal conversation with each patient belonging to the respective plans, informing them that my office was altering our relationship with their insurance companies because the low reimbursements would not allow us to use the superior materials and labs necessary to provide the level of care they deserved. Refusing to compromise *quality* treatment to my valued patients, I went on to tell them that at future appointments they would pay for procedures at the time of their visit and the insurance company would mail them a direct reimbursement. One of my patients summed it up when she said, "Oh no! I don't trust the insurance company to send me my money back." To which I responded by asking, "But it is okay when they do not pay me?" Touché.

Dentists need to come together to resolve the issue of low, delayed reimbursements, by uniting and refusing to sign up for these plans. I know you are thinking that with the economy as it is, staying in network is the safe way to be assured insurance-driven patients ... or better put, remain hostage! I do not know of any other way to inspire change from the superpower if not by refusing to join. If you choose to stay in contracts, it is imperative to educate the patient to understand that insurance is just a percentage off the fee, and, NO, it never covers 100% of anything!

93

Something for Nothing

One morning, my office administrator had been back to my office numerous times exasperated, throwing her hands in the air exclaiming, "These patients have gone crazy!" Billing had been sent out and phone call after phone call had been irate patients calling about overdue accounts. The crazy part being that they were the ones who owed us. You may be thinking if their portion had been collected at time of service—like I have been preaching throughout—my office wouldn't have this problem. And, you would be correct. The fact is that we always do collect prior to or at time of service, but the issue arises when the patient pays their *estimated co-pay* and insurance does not pay its *estimated portion*, leaving the patient with a balance. I know, I know. Why are we still playing this insurance game? Truth be told, it is hard to get out of it. Patients are led to believe, albeit falsely, that insurance covers everything. Most dentists are afraid to drop the plans for fear that their chairs will be completely empty, and during such tough economic times, they may be right. However, the fact remains that offices completely out of network don't deal with this nonsense.

With all of that said, here is the problem I have with these patients: if you know you had a service provided and you receive a bill, why not just pay it? You know you had the work done and you know you owe the office. The insurance company usually sends an EOB (explanation of benefits) to the patient stating what is owed to the doctor long before our office sends a bill to the patient for the balance. So why call the office, indignant? Why must so many want something for nothing? Why do people even fix their mouths to utter, "Can you just write it off"? No, you idiot! We can't just write it off, because we have bills too! Do you think it's right for us to work all day and then write it off just because you asked? Why should we write off anything? We did the work and you need to pay for it! What if your boss short-changed you for several hours of work and when you approached them for your correct pay he asked, "Can it be a wash?" or, "Can we just write that off?"

I have been to a doctor's office myself and used health insurance before, and I dare say, every time I have a balance after the insurance has been billed, I pay it! After all, I know I went in for the service. What would I look like calling the doctor's office, acting a fool, because my insurance company didn't pay?

94

The Dental Shopper

A dental shopper is a person possessing little or no value for their teeth or dental health, who grabs the yellow pages and dials number after number shopping for the "cheapest" prices for *self-diagnosed* dental services. From the first call, the team member should identify that this is not a patient the practice needs and this initial phone call is the best time to weed them out. I do not recommend giving price quotes over the phone, the doctor should always see the patient in person to diagnose and prescribe the necessary treatment. However, in the case of the dental shopper, prices should be given in an effort to dissuade them from coming to the office and wasting precious time.

Allow me to demonstrate how easily identifiable the dental shopper is from the initial call:

Ring! Ring! Ring!

Receptionist: *Divine Dentistry, this is Pam, how may I help you?*

Dental Shopper: *I need to make an appointment... but how much are your cleanings?*

Receptionist: *Okay, we can certainly take care of scheduling. Have you been to our office before?*

Dental Shopper: *No, I saw Dr. Teague in an ad and I want to come in for a cleaning.*

Receptionist: *Okay Ms. Shopper, the first appointment will need to be set with Dr. Teague prior to cleaning. Dr. Teague requires x-rays and will also do a comprehensive examination –*

Dental Shopper: (raising voice) *But I don't need x-rays, just a cleaning!*

Receptionist: *At your first appointment, the doctor will carry out a comprehensive examination, x-rays, and prescribe the cleaning and treatment that is necessary.*

Dental Shopper: *Well, I am sure your prices are too high and I've never been to any office where it costs a lot. Do I have to get all the x-rays?*

When a patient is like this on the phone, she is usually argumentative and disgruntled toward recommended treatment when she presents at the office. My solution for this is very simple, people: tell the patient in your sweetest indoor voice, "Go somewhere else!" How hard is it? You don't go to Nordstrom and expect Wal-Mart prices – not that there is anything wrong with Wal-Mart – the fact remains that there are many "cheaper" offices this patient could go to. Why, then, do they come to yours only to complain about how expensive it is and accuse you of overcharging? Claiming their previous dentist did this or that and was much cheaper, or, denying your diagnosis of periodontal disease because no one ever told them they had it before (shame on them). Nobody is forcing Ms. Cheapskate to come to your office, if a patient or potential patient does not like any aspect of it – pricing, etc., they have the option to go elsewhere. And if you train your office manager, he or she should be able to gently persuade them to do just that.

95

Purpose... Or Shall I Say Lack Thereof?

As healthcare professionals, we feel obligated to treat every person who walks in the door... But, guess what? You don't have to! The beauty of our profession is that we can choose to treat—or not treat—any patient. You should never have anyone in your office that makes the entire team's tummies churn at the site of their name on the schedule. Some people simply are not pleasant. No matter how good, precise, or nice you are, you need to face it: Not everybody will like you... And that's fine!

It is important for the office to know its purpose with every detail spelled out, from the kind of patients the office wants to see, to the atmosphere that the team—including the doctor—wants to work in. The entire team should have a hand in developing it, and it should clearly delineate the parameters by which the office flows. Use your purpose to determine what type of patients and what kind of office YOU desire. Yes, your office has a choice. The following was my office's Purpose Statement:

Purpose

It is our purpose at this office to provide quality dental services, to educate patients on the importance of oral health, and to give patients beautiful smiles that they can be confident about. We exist to serve our patients. When we adhere to our standards, we know that all else will fall into place. Our efforts and treatment will exceed the expectations of those who seek us!

We work in a highly professional and profitable atmosphere and enjoy treating our valued patients. We will go above and beyond the norm for people who want, value, and appreciate our services.

You should re-evaluate any patient that falls outside of your guidelines or purpose for your practice.

96

But I Want to Talk to Dr. Teague

Have you ever had patients call front desk personnel and ask to speak to the doctor? When the doctor picks up, the patient says, "I was referred by Ms. Happy and I would like to make an appointment?" ... or, "I have a question about the bill I received?" ... or, "I thought my insurance covered two cleanings a year" ... etc.

Instances also occur when visitors come to the office, unscheduled, and demand to see the doctor. Such interruptions may be in the form of patients, salespeople, or even solicitors. People have been brazen enough to call the office and say, "I am returning Dr. Teague's call", only for me to get to the phone and have someone I have never heard of, and most definitely not called, try to sell me a service.

When treating patients, I tend to go into a mode. I have been that way since my early years of residency. Once I enter the treatment room, I do not like to be disturbed. I don't want to hear about a person on the phone who wants to talk to me, a person out front who just stopped by, or a person who has a question about a bill (in fact the billing person always knows more about billing than the doctor). My family and close friends know this about me, so they do not call the office unless in an extreme emergency or they contact me on my cell phone. The way I see it is the patient I am treating is paying for this time with me, and that shouldn't be halted. Also, stopping numerous times for interruptions puts one behind, and I don't like to keep patients waiting.

Train your team to handle office visitors. Train them to train your patients. Fewer interruptions allow for a more productive and tranquil environment.

97

I Hate to Bother You, But...

Amazing the number of patients who will call you over the weekend on the emergency line with, "I hate to bother you, but..." Anytime the dialogue begins with that line, you can bet your last dollar it is not an emergency! An emergency is just that, an emergency, and an after-business-hours phone number should be used for emergencies only! I don't know about you, but when I get home, I don't have dentistry on the brain. In fact I think it's safe to say that most people don't want to be reminded of work when they are away from the job. Have you ever had anyone call you on the emergency line to make an appointment? Or call you excessively because their temporary crown came off while eating Laffy-Taffy—the same person you gave strict instructions to stay away from sticky or hard foods to prevent dislodging of the temporary restoration? Or keep calling and/or text messaging about what to expect when you've gone over post-operative instructions numerous times with them? And my all-time favorite, have you ever had someone call you on a Sunday afternoon to talk to you about a delinquent account?

The longer I practice dentistry, the more I realize that most people want what they want when they want it; a direct result of what our society has become, living in the freest country in the world with all of its conveniences and instant gratifications. Gone are the days when the doctor was respected for his time, advice, and expertise. We now live in a world where information is literally at our fingertips, and suffice it to say, everybody becomes their own *"Dr. Search Engine."* This type of *"Internet MD"* research coupled with the public's desire to dictate their individual treatment plans usually forgoes—and certainly undermines—all of the years of study and training it took to become their doctor in the first place.

But back to the subject at hand: patients who call the emergency line for non-emergencies, such as billing or accounts questions... Only recently was I off enjoying my weekend when a message came in via the emergency line. Returning her call within the hour, I learned that Ms. Emergency did not have an emergency at all. Ms. Emergency had a billing question. I can login to my office computer remotely (not necessarily a good thing) allowing me to view a patient's ledger, which of course I did; and to make a long story short, the patient had a balance that was over ninety-days past due and had been turned over to collections by my office administrator.

Ms. Emergency did have a very good track record of fulfilling her financial obligations with our office, and in this particular incident, some issues had arisen with her insurance company that resulted in them paying our office late. But after the insurance payment was made, a significant and aged balance remained. Ms. Emergency complained that my "new girl" would not let her talk to me about her bill and she knew I did not get the message (she was correct, I did not) and she did not want to go to another dentist, but...

Now we all know there is a reason the office administrator did not summon me to discuss an aged account; if she came to me with every person who did not pay their bill, there wouldn't be any time to see patients! Doctors, we have a support team to handle accounts and we must trust them to do so. When working with patients for years upon years, there is a tendency to forge a bond that may be stronger than that of patient-doctor, but at the same time, it is a business and must be run as such. In the past, I have had front office people who were more than lax, allowing favorite patients to have treatments completed and pay later. This results in the office performing many procedures and not getting paid for them. Solution? Explain this to the patient.

"Ms. Emergency, I value our relationship over the years, but I must inform you that my office administrator is simply doing the job that I have asked her to do. She rarely discusses account balances with me, as this is her area of expertise, and in doing so, she would prevent me from actively treating patients. All overdue balances are treated the same, and we would not be in business if we did not collect for the services rendered. I do hope you will continue to be a patient at the office, as you are one of my favorite patients. I will speak with my office administrator to set up financial arrangements for you and get you back on the book as soon as possible."

This approach allows the patient to be heard, which is what most people really want, while holding them accountable for their financial responsibilities. It also allows your team to do their job properly. I don't know if it solves the problem of patients calling after hours for a non-emergency. Sometimes patients abuse the fact that they have access to your private emergency number, but the flip side is that they trust you enough and feel close enough to you to call in the first place. One of the beautiful things about dentistry is that there are not many situations that require immediate attention after hours. Of course, as professionals, we always want to be available to help our valued patients in the event of an unforeseen incident, which is why it is very important to have a vehicle of communication for after hours. Some offices utilize answering services that then forward messages to the doctor, but I have always provided a mobile number for patients of record with emergencies to contact me. I do have patients who call for the heck of it, and the best thing that I've found in this situation is to kindly answer all questions when these calls come and continue to try to prepare patients of what to expect while in the office.

98

Those Who Won't Hold
Their Head Quite right

I know this might seem a bit trivial, but have you ever had a patient who won't hold her head quite right?

Imagine this: You are trying to prep tooth #15, the second maxillary molar, in my opinion the most challenging tooth to treat for a right-handed provider. The tooth seems like it's all the way back to the tonsils and Ms. Trismus can't keep her mouth open and keeps shutting down... and gagging... and crying... and whining. Patiently you say, "Open"... "Open wide".... "Wider" ... "Stay open please". Trying to stabilize the mandible while suctioning, your assistant also blows a gentle stream of air on your mirror to help you see as you continue to try to prep the distal aspect of this tooth. The water from your hand-piece is flying onto the mirror, reminiscent of driving a car in the middle of a hurricane, and you begin to think that you may need some Rain X. Entertaining jokes aside, you desperately want the patient to cooperate so that you can finish the procedure and get her out of her misery. At last, you're done and you all give a sigh of relief. Exhausting! Both you and your assistant were bent like pretzels trying to gain access, while Ms. Trismus had her head retracted like a turtle throughout the whole procedure. Why must it be so difficult?

The Ms. Trismus's certainly make me greatly appreciate the many patients who come in with a smile and are troopers from start to finish. Always thank cooperative patients by ending the treatment with a spunky, "thank you for being such a great patient"... and, "it makes our jobs so easy with wonderful patients like you." They may think its flattery, but you will know it is genuine gratitude. Now don't get me wrong, I appreciate all of my patients and you should too! Without our patients there would be NO practice.

What about the Ms. Trismus's? Well, there are things you can do to help such patients. To help her relax—and lose the turtleneck!—offer her a nice blanket, some headphones, and/or sunglasses to shield the overhead light from her eyes. Use a bite block to aid in keeping her mouth open and prevent closing. Use a rubber dam to prevent the tongue from dancing and the water from the hand-piece pooling in the back of her mouth, thus preventing the gag reflex. The rubber dam, of course, also prevents contamination of the materials being used and provides contrast allowing you to work a bit faster. Most importantly, just be nice to her. Have patience with your patients... it works!

99

But All You Do is Clean Teeth

At the time of writing this, I had been practicing dentistry for twelve years... *twelve!* The time had flown by. Throughout the years, I had many patients come in and say, "You have it easy! You make so much money and all you do is clean teeth." REALLY? ... I mean, *REALLY.* I don't even clean teeth, my #@$! hygienist does! Do people really think I went to school for eight years, majored in the sciences (zoology with a chemistry minor), earned a doctorate degree and then took out a small fortune in loans just to clean their teeth? I mean, *REALLY!!!*

Don't get me wrong, I employ a great hygienist, but with all that goes on behind the scenes, comments like that don't sit well. In my mind, I am thinking, all I do is run the damn practice, sign the checks, work on patients, get screwed by insurance companies, deal with fears, phobias and prejudices, and meet with reps (some of who would sell a used lemon of a car to their own grandmother) etc., all while being underpaid.

Venting to one of my colleagues recently about one of the many dental issues that crop up from day to day, I blurted out, "I don't pay me enough to deal with this!" We both fell apart roaring with laughter, unable to contain ourselves. Laughter. Don't flip the switch. Deal with common ignorance with friendly laughter.

100

They Are Just Teeth!!!!

I loathe hearing patients say, "they are just teeth, pull them all". Err, no. Teeth are highly important for mastication (hello?! – *eating!*), phonetics (umm – *talking!*), and aesthetics (you look fabulous!). They are NOT *just* teeth! Years later, this same person will rue the day they had their precious dentition removed, as their quality of life will be significantly lessened. Unable to enjoy food as much, they will also look years their senior. But, whether we like it or not, people *can* function without teeth.

As artists and doctors who specialize in oral care, they are not just teeth to us, but wondrous living units that help the amazing human body to function harmoniously. The best we can do, is do our best - improving and enhancing the lives of our patients, and, as my office purpose statement aptly sums it up: create smiles that they can be confident about!

Conclusion

The 100 Things I ***HATE****/Love* About Dentistry...

Yes, it is a love/hate, or hate/love relationship. Over the years I have come to realize what is important to me. Deep down I think I always knew, but there was always an intensity deep within to achieve. I have hired and worked with some of the top consultants in the country. At the beginning phase with my last consultant, I had to complete an extensive Q & A. While soul searching to answer some of those questions, I discovered what was truly most important to me.

Different things motivate people. Some people are motivated by money, others status, or a multitude of other things. My motivation, I believe, was achievement. A chronic over-achiever, I launched my solo practice with a one-track mind: I dreamt of an upscale practice doing high-end procedures. I had worked in many offices and I wanted something better, something different. Investing an enormous amount of revenue and energy in continuing education courses - not the minimum courses required to maintain my license, but courses well beyond what was required by state boards. It was not unusual for me to have over 100 hours of continuing education courses per year when state requirements were a mere 20. I wanted a different type of practice. I wanted the large, complicated cases that the average dentist couldn't handle. I wanted the cosmetic case that would change a person's personality, enhance his/her confidence and, in essence, change his/her life. And yes, I wanted to be compensated for these cases. After all, I invested a small fortune to produce this "high-end dentistry."

With each phase of dentistry, I found that I became more and more consumed by it. Sure, I was always *trying* to become better - I used consultants because I wanted to have a better business model and give patients a better dental experience, and I took advanced courses at leading institutions so I could be the best clinician. And yes, I did well, but was this making me happy? I hired and worked with some of the top consultants in the country, yet no matter how well I did, it never felt good enough. When I launched

161

my practice in 2004, my lending agency required borrowers to participate in a system they called "practice heartbeat"; a program where each month for the first year of practice, you were required to call in and go over the numbers and statistics from your office. It was a way for the company to monitor your practice progress and ensure that you would be able to honor your obligations to pay them back. One day while on the phone with my representative going over the previous month's numbers/financials, I found myself highly disappointed and expressed my frustration, "I wanted to do so much better than this. I didn't reach *my* goals! I expected this month to be so much better!" The representative cut in, and I will never forget what she said, "Hold up! Don't beat yourself up, you are—and continue to be—in the black during your first year. That is unheard of. I monitor practices all over the country and you are doing better than the majority of startup practices. Cut yourself some slack and give yourself some credit."

Fast forward from then to several years ago when I worked with my last consultant. Filling out their detailed Q&A, I discovered what was truly important to me. It was never about money or status, which came as no surprise given neither has ever impressed me. But each question I answered indicated a severe imbalance... all my answers showed a desire for family life. I grew up—and still was—very close to my family, but at this point in my life I was single and had no family of my own. I never realized, prior to answering those questions, that I felt a void. My whole world was consumed with "my office". Oh sure, I dated, but was not finding the right kind of life mate. I think that by putting more time and effort in to my practice I had a sense of control. If things were haphazard, I could always work harder. If business was slow, I could market more, and yes, work harder. If the economy was headed south... you guessed it, I could work harder! Of course, through the years I figured out how to work smarter, but the point is that though I could control "my office", I could *not* control if or when I would meet a suitable mate. And, that was true to a certain extent.

Of course, my goal to have a better practice model, run a more efficient business, improve customer service, and be compensated well remained absolute. But as I answered those questions some four years ago, I realized where my priorities had been misappropriated. And with this realization, I began to make life changes. Adopting the philosophy of my consultants of putting life first and letting the office follow suit, I started taking vacations—

four weeks per year—yes, I said four! Something unmentionable before, it turned out these breaks allowed me to be more creative. The practice did better and I *felt* better. I had balance and I was receiving a new life. Recently, I married my soul mate. This may never have happened had I stayed on the rat treadmill and kept "working harder".

This book has been cathartic—*therapeutic*—to me. The idea came to me following years and years of practicing while hearing a voice in my head saying, "I hate this." People say God talks to you and I am sure you have also heard His voice... like a whisper, then a nudge, and then an all and out *scream!* Why don't we listen? The sign may not always come as a James Earl Jones voiceover, like heard in the movies, but it is a sign nonetheless. The funny thing is I would literally hear this voice in my head every time I entered the treatment room to start a procedure. While the voice sounded like my own—kind of like when you are thinking to yourself— I couldn't quiet it. It kept on and on, and became louder and louder. I kept telling myself, "I cannot *hate* this! I went to school way too many years and borrowed far too much money to pursue this career! I cannot *hate* this, as it's all I ever said I was going to do since the ripe age of five! I cannot *hate* this! I am educated and well trained... I am an *expert!* Besides, what else could I possibly do?" One day, unsuccessfully trying to ignore the voice, I instead surrendered to it and went to my office and began writing all of my thoughts down. Boom! It came to me, *The 100 Things I HATE/Love About Dentistry.* Any time I heard the voice, instead of silencing it – or trying to - I wrote in my journal. Whenever I had a difficult day or a challenging procedure, the words would flow like lava and I would complete chapters in mere minutes. Did this mean that I hated what I had always aspired to do? I don't think so.

This resulting book is a message to dental and health care professionals that you are not alone, that other practitioners feel just like you. It doesn't mean you–or I!—do not love what we do; it means that we are human. It means it is okay to not know all the answers, and it is okay to seek help, whether via study clubs or business consultants. I believe God was whispering to me all those years ago. As it became louder and louder, I realized He was giving me these words to help guide others to live a better quality of life.

With the play on words–hate—we should always focus on what we love, on what our true purpose is and our priorities are. We should focus on what truly fulfills us. I chose the word hate in an effort to grab your attention while providing positive solutions to daily rigors, but I don't want to lose sight of the so many things that I love. Such as the three year old patient I saw many years ago who would come in and give me the biggest hug and then make excuses to her mom and dad to "Go back to see the dentist" before her six months checkup was due. Or the patient who cried when I did a smile design (cosmetic case) because her confidence level had dramatically changed now that she can smile. Or the patient who would bring in homemade soap because she loved my dental team, or, the one who comes in and says, "I'm just so proud of you" or "You know, I just want to say thank you because you do a great job". In our lives we hear so much negativity on the news and in general that small gestures like these make it all worthwhile.

I hope that this read has lifted your spirits and inspired you in some way. Always know that you can practice dentistry a better way. Success and happiness are not disparate; you can—and should aspire to—enjoy both.

Bonus

Common Sense Ain't So Common

Some things do not need to be spelled out. Really? You would be surprised... Over the years I have learned from experience not to take the level of common sense a person possesses for granted. The following list is made up of some common sense rules I created based on direct experiences. As you will see, common sense ain't so common. So if you are in doubt, always S-P-E-L-L it out.

- Never EVER enter a treatment room and speak over the patient about another patient!

- Don't enter the doctor's personal office (without chart information and date of birth) saying Dr. X's office is on the phone with a question about Ms. Tooth Ache that we referred to him two months ago! *How the heck do I remember Ms. Tooth Ache? I have only seen about 250 other mouths since her appointment. And, there may be more than one Ms. Tooth Ache in the computer. People do often have the same name as somebody else.*

- Do not talk about your personal business, baby daddy etc. at the front desk! *Patients in the reception area can hear you.*

- Do not chew gum at work! Can you say UNPROFESSIONAL?

- If your office has two entrances, do not come through the main patient entrance if you are late!

- It is not okay to let a patient walk out the door without paying on the procedure they just had! *Shall I take that out of your check?*

- It is not okay to remove money from the petty cash drawer and leave an I.O.U. note in its place!

- It is inappropriate to ask and no, I cannot lend you money. *NO, not even for a house so you can flip it and we both make a small fortune!*

- It is not okay to interrupt the doctor during patient treatment because there is a solicitor who wants to sell something upfront! Or someone dropped by who says he went to high school with the doctor! True emergencies only are the only acceptable reason to disrupt the doctor during patient treatment.

- It is not okay to show up for an interview an hour late, chewing gum and wearing tennis shoes!

About the Author

Dr. Evelyn Teague Samuel is the owner of Evelyn F. Teague D.M.D. P.C., and Teague Principles, LLC. For eight years she did business under the name of, and was the creative force behind, Park Place Dentistry, a practice launched from conception with her trademark vision and fortitude. Graduating with honors from Alabama Agricultural and Mechanical University with a Bachelors of Science degree in Zoology in 1995, Dr. Samuel received her Doctor of Dental Medicine degree from the University of Alabama School of Dentistry in 1999. This was followed by a post-doctoral residency in Advanced Education in General Dentistry at Howard University College of Dentistry.

Achieving her lifetime goal of becoming a dentist, Dr. Samuel set out to provide excellence within her chosen field. Committing numerous hours to continuing education each year, such as advanced cosmetic and neuromuscular dental studies at the world renowned Las Vegas Institute for Advanced Dental Studies, she is always at the forefront of new and cutting-edge technology.

During her eight years as a solo practitioner and practice owner, Dr. Samuel ran a highly efficient office achieving record growth, productivity, and a 98% collection rate. Statistical analyses comparing Park Place Dentistry to practices within Alabama and adjacent states consistently revealed a performance level far surpassing many other dental offices.

Dr. Samuel's passion for the art of dentistry, coupled with her highly skilled and trained eye for detail and natural gift of running an efficient business makes her a sought-after entity by colleagues and other business owners. Dr. Samuel simply knows what works! Aided by her strong attention to detail and conditions, she is an ultra-effective coach, guiding and inspiring efficiency and success in their respective businesses.

A member of several dental organizations including the American Dental Association and the American Academy of Cosmetic Dentistry, Dr. Samuel takes great pride in enhancing smiles, changing the lives of her patients, and helping colleagues to obtain their ideal practices. In addition, she is a featured doctor in the book, *The Art of Creating Practice Success* by Dr. Bill and Carolyn Blatchford (Blatchford Blueprints, Copyright 2009). In her spare time, Dr. Samuel enjoys reading, traveling, exercise, and spending time with her loving husband, James.

CPSIA information can be obtained at www.ICGtesting.com
Printed in the USA
LVOW121935190513

334452LV00003B/4/P

9 780988 980402